PSYCHIC BLESSINGS

by Diane Lazarus
with Linda Dearsley

This edition first published in paperback by
Michael Terence Publishing in 2022
www.mtp.agency

Copyright © 2022 Diane Lazarus

Diane Lazarus has asserted the right to be identified as
the author of this work in accordance with the
Copyright, Designs and Patents Act 1988

ISBN 9781800944152

No part of this publication may be reproduced, stored
in a retrieval system, or transmitted, in any form or
by any means, electronic, mechanical, photocopying,
recording or otherwise, without the prior
permission of the publisher

Cover images
Copyright © Azgek www.123rf.com
and
courtesy of Diane Lazarus

Cover design
Copyright © 2022 Michael Terence Publishing

One

It was Saturday morning and there we were, my husband Peter and me, side by side in our lovely comfy bed, having a lie-in. We didn't often get the chance to be lazy but Peter needed a rest, I thought. He'd been so stressed lately.

Something really bad was going on with his solicitor's practice, I knew it. He was always on the phone chasing up money, or rushing anxiously here and there to mysterious meetings. Yet he wouldn't share the problem with me. Even though he believed in my psychic gifts, he wouldn't confide. 'Don't worry Di,' he always said. 'It's getting sorted. Everything'll be fine.'

And though I could have used my abilities to discover more, it wasn't right to pry. You shouldn't use your powers to spy on people uninvited, I'd been told.

But this morning was different. For once Peter actually wanted my help. Something seemed to have changed.

'Diane,' he said suddenly, turning towards me on his pillow, 'would you do a reading for me? I really need a reading.'

His face had gone oddly intense. He sounded quite desperate. 'I *need* you to read me,' he insisted, 'I really need to see where I'm going in my future.'

My future? Shouldn't that be *our* future? I remember thinking vaguely, the beginnings of an alarm bell stirring in my mind.

Still, I was always saying I wanted to help so I could hardly refuse him now. 'Ok. No problem,' I said lightly, but inside I had the nastiest feeling I was going to regret this.

I turned to look at the blank wall, the way I always do when I visualise for people. The doomy fingers of foreboding were growing stronger but I shut them down, cleared my mind and concentrated on imagining Peter in the future. After a moment, a picture began to form across the bright, white wall opposite the bed, as if an invisible projector was using our wall as a cinema screen.

The figure of a medium-height man, in a short-sleeved white shirt and tie appeared in the centre of the scene. He was brushing back his light brown hair with one hand and putting on sunglasses with the other. It was Peter. He looked tanned and relaxed and he seemed to be waiting for someone. He was standing in front of a very tall, opulently gleaming building. The sun was shining, dazzling-bright and the polished glass of the building acted like a mirror. I could see people reflected in it as they walked by, all dressed in cool, summery clothes. There were further swanky buildings across the road and above it all sweltered a hot, blue sky.

I knew immediately I was looking at a street in Dubai. My daughter Lisa had recently got a job out there and I recognised it from her pictures.

Suddenly a small boy appeared by Peter. A dark-haired little lad with huge brown eyes. Then the scene changed, just like a film. Now the two of them - the little boy and Peter - were in some sort of cricket ground. The boy was holding a cricket bat and slicing bravely at an oncoming ball, while Peter stood nearby, watching him proudly. Strangely enough the boy looked very much the way my teenage son Liam looked, when he was about eight years old.

'I see you going to live in Dubai,' I said slowly to Peter. I didn't say anything about the boy. Despite being the image of my Liam I knew he didn't belong to me.

Relief flooded across Peter's face. Though he'd never expressed any interest in living in Dubai before, he seemed pretty pleased about the idea.

Yet I felt uneasy. I didn't see myself living in Dubai and I didn't see myself having another child either. I'd had to have a hysterectomy years ago after Liam was born and much as I love children, I felt my family was complete.

I stared more carefully at my cinema screen. The scene was changing again and there was Peter walking towards his car, an attractive raven-haired woman at his side. She was slim and exotic looking, and just from the way they moved together, I got the feeling they were close. I hadn't been off beam about the child, I thought to myself. I bet that little boy was Peter's future son and I was probably looking at the boy's mother right there – and it certainly wasn't me.

I pulled my eyes abruptly away from the wall and Dubai started to dissolve. 'I can't see any more,' I fibbed. 'But that's it. Your future is in Dubai.'

'But not with me,' I added silently to myself.

Peter was delighted but I felt icy claws creeping into my stomach. Despite the warm duvet tucked round me, I shivered. My visions were always true, even though, quite often I didn't want to believe them. Peter was the love of my life. After two failed relationships I'd believed I'd found my soulmate at last. But now I knew, this couldn't be true. I was going to be let down - again.

Ever since I won the Channel 5 TV show Britain's Psychic Challenge back in 2006, people often said how wonderful it must be to have this odd ability. To be able to see what's going to happen in the future and also to talk to people who've passed away.

And of course in many ways it *is* wonderful. It gives me so much pleasure to be able to bring hope and happiness to people who're grieving or desperate. I really love my job when I see their faces light up.

Yet if only the people who envy me knew the whole story. It's not always comfortable to be able to glimpse the future. Sometimes the unvarnished truth is hard to take. At times I'd really rather not know.

As I watched the worrying Dubai scenes finally disappear

from the wall I had a sudden flashback to when I was 14 years old.

We were in the middle of a family gathering at Mum's house in Swansea and I looked across the room and caught sight of one of my aunts sitting opposite. In that split second I just knew, instantly, she was having an affair with the man next to her – an old family friend.

How I knew, I had no idea. It just came to me with absolute certainty. The two of them were lovers, no question and it bothered me. It just wasn't right! They were both married to other people for goodness' sake – people I cared about. Betraying loved ones under our very noses.

I brooded about it for quite a while in my idealistic, schoolgirl way. It was so worrying. I didn't want anyone to get hurt. I thought I ought to stop them but how? What could I do? And how could I tell anyone? I had no proof and it seemed so unlikely. They must have been way over 40 after all!

Eventually, when my older brother Gary came home on leave from the Army, I confided in him.

I'd always admired Gary. He was so kind and I knew he wouldn't dismiss me out of hand. But though Gary was sympathetic as ever, he didn't have an answer.

'That's awful Di and you could be right,' he said. 'But you can't say anything. It would cause so much trouble.'

He was right of course. Though, whenever we were all together – which was quite often, I'd look at the two of them, my aunt and that man, laughing and joking and catching each other's eye and it was so obvious to me it was like a siren going off in my head. Surely everyone else could see it too? But somehow, they couldn't.

In the end it nagged at me so much I mentioned it to my mother.

'Don't be stupid Diane,' she said, horrified. 'What an idea!

That's ridiculous. Of course there's nothing going on. That's my sister you're talking about.'

She just didn't want to believe it and of course I couldn't prove what I was saying was true. I couldn't even pretend I'd seen anything suspicious. There was nothing I could do. Yet I knew I was right.

It seemed so unfair. It was just like when I was a small girl and kept seeing people no one else could see. People who weren't there, according to Mum. I wasn't allowed to talk about it.

'You mustn't say these things to anyone Diane,' she'd sa., 'You mustn't talk like that. People will think there's something wrong with you.'

So just like I did then, I kept quiet about the affair. Not that it did me any good. In fact, in the end it was me who got into trouble. Talk about injustice!

It happened like this: one afternoon the two-faced pair were round at our house, smirking together as usual when they thought no one was looking. I turned away in disgust but somehow, as I swung my head I accidentally caught the man's eye. Our gaze met, and held, and in that split second, his expression changed. He saw that I knew. And he saw that I knew he knew.

I gave him my fiercest, most Arctic stare. I had to let him know what I thought of him. If I'd been gifted with different powers, that look would have frozen him to a scrawny iceberg on Mum's swirly carpet in a trice. If only!

Instead, as the others wandered off into the other room, leaving just the two of us alone, he moved towards the door, blocking my exit. I looked up at his face, suddenly angry and hostile. It was clear he loathed me as much as I loathed him. I'd made an enemy that day and, I don't know why, but I started to laugh. Nerves I suppose because it certainly wasn't funny. I couldn't seem to stop laughing. The next second his arm swung out and he slapped me hard across the face. Then he shoved me roughly aside, pushed past and strode swiftly out into the hall as if nothing had happened.

Shocked, my ears ringing, cheek already turning scarlet I ran up to my room, slammed the door and burst into tears. I stayed there the rest of the evening. Next day I woke to a big, fat, black eye. What could I say? I had to tell everyone I'd walked into the wardrobe door.

And that's what being psychic does for you, I thought ruefully now, blinking away the last vestiges of Dubai and climbing out of bed. It's not all glitz and glamour and bouquets of flowers. Sometimes it breaks your heart.

Oh and there was a delayed PS to my schoolgirl story. Eleven years later when I was 25, the truth finally came out. The lovers' secret was discovered and my aunt admitted she'd been having an affair with that man the whole time. I'd been right all along even though no one would believe me.

So now, older and supposedly wiser, I had to swing into my 'knowing but not knowing' mindset. It's difficult to explain, but over the years I'd developed a way of living in the present as if I didn't know what was going to happen in the future – even though I did! I'd learned a knack of shutting my mind to events ahead and concentrating completely on what was happening now. One day at a time became my philosophy – it was the only way to cope.

So I said nothing to Peter about the woman he was going to meet in Dubai and tried to pretend to myself everything was fine.

But it wasn't. Peter remained withdrawn and distant. There was a recession going on, here in Wales it was particularly bad and businesses were failing every day. Numerous companies were having trouble getting the payments they were owed, and it seemed Peter's was no exception.

Sometimes I overheard him on the phone, trying to persuade creditors to settle their bills. Once I even heard the sum of

£47,000 mentioned. My knees went weak at the enormity of it all and I quickly shut the kitchen door so I wouldn't hear any more. There was no way we could find that sort of money. No wonder Peter was worried. People weren't paying him what they should and it was obvious the financial situation was getting serious.

Then a few weeks later, out of nowhere, Peter suddenly announced he'd got a new job – in Dubai – and he had to leave immediately.

'But what about your office… and the staff… your clients?' I said in bewilderment. 'And what about us?'

Liam was still at school, Lisa was away at University in England, I was busy with my psychic work and we'd hardly finished doing up our beautiful new house – my dream house. There was the mortgage to pay, our bills…

Peter's face shut down. 'I'm sorry Di but I've got to go. I've had enough. I can't cope. It's stressing me out too much here. I've got to get away and I've got to earn some money. We can keep in touch on Skype and you and Liam can come out in the holidays. He'll love it. You'll love it. And Lisa's always going over to visit friends out there – she'll love it too.'

'But what about the office?' I insisted. He'd been so proud of his office and his loyal staff. 'Have you told them? Do they know?'

A guilty look flitted across his face.

'You haven't, have you?' I said. 'You haven't told them. You're just walking out on them.'

Peter turned away. He was so stressed he was probably on the edge of a breakdown. He didn't want anyone to know, that was the bottom line. He couldn't cope any more and just wanted to creep away and recover.

'Please don't say anything to anyone Di,' he pleaded. 'It's all being taken care of, I promise. I've got a specialist company sorting everything out. They're chasing up the money I'm owed and they'll assign my cases to other solicitors. You don't need to worry.'

Well I knew that wasn't true. There was every reason to worry. But everything was such a whirl, I felt strangely numb.

Next thing I knew, Peter was flinging clothes into a suitcase, telling Liam what a wonderful time they'd have in the holidays playing cricket, then with a quick, slightly guilty goodbye kiss on my cheek, he was dashing off to the airport and his flight to Dubai. As I watched him hurry away down the path I saw relief written all over his back.

And that was it. I walked back indoors and the emptiness of the big house settled all round me like a big, muffling duvet. Liam had gone to visit his friend. And now heavy silence seeped from every room. Nothing stirred. Here I was, rattling around in the lovely home that was once my dream – all alone.

Of course it wasn't long before the fallout began to come crashing down. Naturally the office staff wondered why Peter hadn't turned up for work on Monday morning. Or Tuesday for that matter. Then his clients wanted to know how their cases were coming along. Every day I came home to a string of increasingly irate messages on the answerphone. Where was Peter? Was he sick? What should they tell the clients?

When was he coming back?

I didn't know what to say. Peter had insisted I say nothing to anyone and anyway – how could I tell them he'd taken another job thousands of miles away from the recession, in Dubai?

At the time we were living in a small village outside Swansea – the sort of place where everyone knew everyone else. It got so I hardly dared pop into a shop for a pint of milk in case someone cornered me wanting to know what was going on.

Gossip began to spread. Heads turned when I drove by and

then plaintive emails began arriving from Peter's anxious office staff. They hadn't been paid, they wrote, and they had young families to feed. When could they expect their wages? It really upset me. I felt so bad. I hated owing money to anyone but there was nothing I could do. We couldn't pay what we didn't have.

'Forget it Diane, it'll be sorted,' Peter assured me every time I tackled him about it. 'I've got a Swansea solicitor to take over all the problems and debts and the open case files, and there's a specialist that dissolves companies winding up my business for me. This kind of thing happens all the time. No need for you to be involved.'

But I *was* involved. It was impossible for Peter to keep track of what the Swansea solicitor was doing from over 4,000 miles away. Meanwhile I was right there in the thick of it; everyone knew I was Peter's wife and they wanted answers. I took to driving to the next town to do my shopping and the rest of the time, I simply raced between home and the small office I rented behind Peter's premises and kept my head down as much as possible.

Yet even in my office I wasn't safe. One day a hefty builder barged into my serene little waiting room and planted himself purple-faced and angry between the coffee table and the door.

'I want paying for the work I've done!' he shouted over the top of my relaxing music, waving his arms around so much he almost knocked over the weeping fig in the corner. Thank goodness I didn't have a client with me just then. 'It's been months now. No more excuses!'

He was so aggressive it was frightening. I glanced past him through the glass door to where my car was parked behind the building. But the builder's muddy pick-up had been driven right up to my bonnet and then left slung at an angle, blocking the exit. There was no escape.

'Well I'm sorry but I'm afraid my husband's away at the moment,' I said as calmly as I could, drawing on the skills I'd learned as a child when my drunken father was rampaging round the flat. Inwardly I was shaking but I kept my face unconcerned as I coolly reached for my phone and hit speed dial. 'Ok, so I'm calling my brother now, he's only up the road. I'll get him over and you can discuss it with him. He's ex-Army.'

'Oh hello, Gary!' I said into the phone as Gary answered, 'Could you come over, right now? I've got an… irate… gentlemen here… wants to talk about a bill and he's blocking my car in. Thanks Gary.' I clicked off the call. 'He'll be right over,' I told the builder.

The man scowled even more threateningly and I thought he was going to smash his meaty fist down on the coffee table.

'You've not heard the last of this!' he bellowed. 'That money better be here by the end of the week!'

And with that, he stomped out, threw himself into the pick-up, slammed the door and roared away.

By the time Gary arrived, I was trembling but unhurt. 'I'm not even sure what work Peter had done,' I said to Gary.

'Well let me know if he turns up again,' said Gary giving me a hug, 'and I'll deal with him. It's not fair to take it out on you.'

Which was true, and there was no excuse for such abusive behaviour, though I could understand why the man was so angry. If he'd done the work Peter had asked for, he deserved to be paid.

It just got worse and worse, but of course there was still money for the mortgage to be found. Well two mortgages actually. When we'd bought my dream home the recession was just starting and we were unable to sell our old farmhouse nearby – so Peter decided it would be a great idea to rent it out to cover the cost. Unfortunately, he let it to an acquaintance who, unknown to Peter, turned out to be suffering from severe depression.

Eventually the poor man walked out and when I went round to see what needed doing before we offered it for rent again, I was horrified. The place was filthy, the furniture broken, most of the windows so dirty you could hardly see out of them and others smashed. It turned out the miserable tenant had been living in one darkened room like a wounded animal in its lair.

I had to scrub the place from top to bottom, throw out the broken furniture, re-paint every room and hack down the tangle of weeds that had sprung up like Sleeping Beauty's castle all around our once pretty home. I could have cried. It was so comfortable when we lived there. Now it was a wreck. Still, despite it all, both mortgages had to be paid, plus the household bills and our food. It was all down to me and whatever Peter could send from Dubai.

I took on as much work as I could humanly manage, sold my beloved little sports car and used my life savings plus the earnings from the sale of my first book, Mixed Blessings – in which I tell the story of how my baffling gift developed during my troubled childhood. And still it wasn't enough.

One day there was a knock on the door and I opened it to find a stranger standing on the doorstep. Round his neck was a laminated ID card and straight away my eyes went to the words 'Inland Revenue' clearly printed across the front. My mouth went dry and I had to stop my hands from shaking.

'Is Mr Lazarus in?' asked the official – perfectly politely to be fair.

'No,' I said. 'I'm afraid not and I don't know when he'll be back.'

The official didn't look too surprised. 'Well, if you speak to him, would you tell him to call this number? It's urgent.' He handed me a card.

'Yes of course,' I said, quickly.

The man gave me a long, shrewd stare, probably thinking that phone call was never going to happen but he'd done his job.

Then with a tiny shrug, he turned and went back to his car.

Shocked, I closed the door and sank down on the stairs, the horrible, uncaring card still clutched in my hand. So now there must be an unpaid tax bill. A big bill at that. They wouldn't come all the way to your house for just a couple of pounds.

Suddenly the years fell away and I was ten again and my violent, alcoholic father was stomping round the house, stripping out every piece of furniture we possessed. As he loaded it all into a van, Mum, my brothers and sister Debbie barricaded themselves in the bedroom Debbie and I shared. After he'd gone, Mum was left with nothing. When the gas and electricity were cut off, Mum filled the house with candles and cooked our meals on a camping stove - only, often, there were no meals to cook as she'd run out of money for food.

Unbelievable! I thought now, staring again at the taxman's card. It's history repeating itself. Despite all my hard work, despite everything I've done, I'm going to end up just like Mum. And tears began to splash down onto the little white square.

'No you're not...' said a quiet voice in front of me.

I looked up. Liam was at school. The house was empty: I was quite alone.

Yet in the shadows in the corner of the hall I could make out the faint outline of a man.

'Don't worry child,' he said gently. 'Everything's going to be alright. You'll be fine.'

I recognised that voice. I stared at the indistinct shape, trying to see him better. At least I finally knew who he was. It was my great, great grandfather, the railway pioneer Ronald O. Preston, the amazing man who'd built a railway right across Kenya a century ago. He'd been watching over me since I was a tiny toddler.

Back then I'd called him the 'Lined Man' because I didn't

know who he was and his face was so marked by the harsh African sun it seemed to be made of lines. His appearance looked so strange to me then, I was frightened, but gradually over the years I understood he was protecting me - he'd always been protecting me - and the fear faded away.

'I don't see how,' I sniffed, out loud now. How could I be fine with all this going on? The debts and the difficulties were just impossible.

'Trust! Don't worry,' he said again. 'Everything will work out as it should. You'll be alright.'

And with that, the blurry figure melted away and the shadows were just empty shadows again.

Though suddenly I didn't feel quite so alone. My great, great grandfather had never let me down before. He'd always been there, watching over me when life got tough. Well it was certainly tough now. But he never lied. So if he said everything was going to be alright, lord knows how, but it was going to be alright.

Two

'Diane!'

Walking through Dubai airport pulling along my suitcase with one hand and steering Liam with the other, I'd been marvelling at the laden Christmas trees amongst the potted palms and the hot sun blazing through the glass. December was never like this in Swansea!

'Diane!' shouted the voice again.

'Mum, there's Peter!' said Liam at the same moment. I looked round and suddenly I saw him. Leaning across the arrivals barrier, waving frantically, his face all welcoming smiles.

And I have to admit, tiny butterflies leapt and fizzed inside at the sight of him. This was the man I loved after all, despite everything. I hadn't seen him for months and now here he was, bronzed, fit and looking happier than he had for... goodness knows how long. At least a year, I realised. That terrible strained look around his eyes had faded away and now he appeared boyish, enthusiastic and full of energy.

I hurried towards him and we folded into a big hug.

'It's so good to see you!' said Peter taking my case from me and giving me an extra squeeze. 'Come on. Did you have a good flight? Are you hungry? The car's outside.'

Luckily Peter's new job had come with a company car. Nothing special – just a modest little run-around but it was perfect for his needs in the city.

Peter led us expertly through the holiday crowds out into the dazzling desert sun, the three of us chattering happily the whole way.

We were in Dubai for a month. Peter had presumably scraped

up every last penny from his new wages for the plane tickets and there was no point in ruining Liam's holiday with arguments about the problems at home. So I tried to ignore my anger at the mess and once again concentrate on living in the present.

In the end, Liam and I did have a nice enough trip. Peter was working during the day and some weekends so we were on our own a lot of the time but when he was back I tried to ignore everything that was going on in Wales and just enjoy myself.

After all Peter wasn't a bad person: he'd been a wonderful father to Lisa and Liam and we'd enjoyed many happy times together as a couple. He was genuinely pleased to see me, and really, when I could forget the trouble back home, I was pleased to see him too.

So whenever he had a moment to spare, Peter showed us the sights. Dubai was fascinating, genuinely jaw-dropping – all those extravagant buildings diamond bright against the brilliant sky. Plus of course it was wonderful to get away from the cold and soak up some winter sunshine.

Yet while we were enjoying Christmas by a sparkling sea - incredibly, our financial situation was getting even worse. Before I'd left home, I'd been busy redecorating the farmhouse, ready to rent out, hopefully, in the New Year to help pay the mortgage. I'd just about put the finishing touches in when it was time to leave for Dubai, so I phoned Peter to bring him up to speed: 'The farmhouse looks lovely now,' I said. 'You wouldn't believe the difference. But Peter, it's going to get really cold here over Christmas. Don't forget to pay the insurance.'

'Course not,' said Peter, but rather off-handedly I thought. As if he wasn't really listening.

'No, really Peter,' I said seriously, 'I've got a feeling. You will pay it won't you?'

'For goodness' sake Diane,' he said, mock-scolding. 'It's all in hand. Just get yourself over here and stop worrying! Get on the plane!'

I did try not to worry. But all the time there was this tiny little pip of anxiety niggling inside.

Anyway, finally our holiday was over and it was time to go home. Peter begged me to stay, to move out there permanently with him, but how could I? Liam was doing well at school with important exams coming up and I had a lot of work booked. Besides, of course, our affairs in Wales were in a dreadful mess to put it mildly. Someone had to be on hand to sort it all out.

'It's impossible Peter,' I told him firmly. 'We'll just have to see how it goes.'

It was cold and wet when we got back to Swansea, quite late on a dark winter evening, but the decorations were still up, twinkling lights everywhere and it felt right somehow. Exciting as Dubai had been, Christmas in the desert just wasn't the same.

'It's freezing, but isn't it nice to have seasons?' I said to Liam as we headed home.

'Just what I was thinking Mum,' he agreed. Every day seemed the same in Dubai and after a while you start to long for something a bit different. Liam and I did, anyway.

Despite the problems it was good to be back and wonderful to sink into my own bed. Yet oddly enough, that night I couldn't sleep. The farmhouse kept leaping into my mind every time I closed my eyes and I was getting more and more wound up. Something was wrong there, I knew it.

As soon as it was light I leapt up, threw on some old clothes and raced over to our former home. From the outside it looked just as I'd left it but as I walked up the path the feeling of dread got stronger and stronger.

My hands were shaking as I turned the key in the lock and apprehensively pushed open the front door.

Instantly a musty, damp smell hit me in the face like a slap. Then my eyes focused on the sodden carpet and sprays of spotty mould already marching across my newly painted walls. I squelched further inside. Ceiling paper hung almost to the floor, piles of soggy plaster lay in heaps and disintegrated under foot, and in places when I looked up I could see right through to the bedrooms above.

You didn't need to be clairvoyant to guess what had happened. The pipes in the attic had frozen at some point during the holiday, then burst and water had poured through the ceilings into the bedrooms and then right through the bedrooms into the lounge below, taking part of the ceiling with it for good measure.

The whole place was ruined.

Trembling from head to foot, I pulled out my phone and rang Peter.

'Would you text me the insurance details?' I asked when I'd explained what had happened. 'They'll have to get someone out to assess the damage.'

'Call you back,' said Peter abruptly.

Well he needed to find the documents and write down the reference numbers I reasoned. It seemed to take him ages – which was odd as he was normally meticulous with his paperwork - but finally the phone rang.

'Di I don't know how to tell you this,' said Peter slowly. 'I'm so sorry, but I forgot to renew the insurance. We're not insured… it ran out two months ago…'

I'd like to say I couldn't believe it, but to tell the truth, by now, I could – I could believe it only too well.

'But Peter I warned you! I told you I had a feeling,' I cried. 'I asked you before I came out and you said you'd paid!'

'I know, I know,' Peter agreed, 'I meant to do it, I really did… but I forgot. I've been so busy…'

Busy?! At that, I was so upset, I cut off the call. I couldn't bring myself to speak to him.

The phone rang again several times but I refused to pick up. I didn't want to talk about it. What was the use of excuses?

Back home, the awful scenes in the farmhouse kept flashing before my eyes and I couldn't keep the tears back. Seemed like I was always crying these days. I felt so helpless. Everything I tried to do, no matter how hard I worked, just seemed to go wrong. I didn't know which way to turn. It was like one of those nightmares where you're trying to run but your feet are stuck in glue and no matter how you struggle, you can't get anywhere.

I sobbed and sobbed. Suddenly there was a gentle hand on my shoulder. 'Dry your eyes girl.' said that familiar voice, and straight away I could feel the comforting presence of my great, great grandfather standing beside me again, though this time I couldn't see him. 'It will be alright. Didn't I tell you? Everything will turn out fine, you'll see. Help is coming. Trust.'

And just like before, he melted away.

It was difficult to believe, particularly when I got a quote from a local builder to repair the house and it came to £25,000 – completely impossible for me to find. Although strangely, I did feel comforted by his words and amazingly, little by little things did begin to improve.

First Peter's parents kindly offered to help with the tax bill. Then one evening at the meditation class I ran to try to raise extra funds, I happened to mention the disaster zone that was our farmhouse. Immediately, one of my students, a sympathetic young man named Michael, reminded me he was a builder. What's more, he was between jobs at that point as the recession was still affecting us.

'That quote you got sounds a bit over the top Di,' he said. 'I could probably work you out a much better deal.'

Sure enough, after checking the damage, he agreed to do the work for a fraction of the previous builder's price. He even agreed Peter could pay in instalments from his wages in Dubai so I didn't have to worry about finding the money.

Suddenly it was like I had a fairy godmother! A few days later my sister Debbie and I were having a catch up on the phone. I was telling her all about the leak and the state of the farmhouse, plus the fact that we weren't insured.

'Why couldn't it have happened here?' I joked, looking round at my once dream home, the place Peter had so rapidly abandoned, 'The insurance's all paid up and I've never liked that old carpet in the hall!'

'Yeah and those tiles you'd like instead would cost a fortune!' teased Debbie.

'I could do with a new sofa too!' I giggled.

We went on and on, having a good laugh and come the end of our chat I was smiling. By the time I put the phone down I was feeling much better. Good old Debbie, I said to myself as I went into the kitchen to put the kettle on. She always cheers me up! And I thought no more about it.

A few months later I came downstairs one morning and stepped straight into a pool of water. Baffled, I paddled up the hall, following the water upstream until I arrived in the lounge where a shallow lake engulfed the sofa, seeped into Liam's laptop where he'd been doing his homework the night before and dripped off the TV.

It was the strangest thing. I couldn't work out where the water was coming from. I phoned Mike and he downed tools at the farmhouse at once to come to the rescue again. Eventually the mystery was solved. Turned out our house had been fitted with one of the earliest forms of underfloor heating – well, since the Romans anyway! It involved plastic hoses filled with hot water coiled beneath the floorboards where no one could see them. Somehow, during the night one of them had unaccountably split and been quietly pumping out warm water while we slept.

Oddly, only the two rooms I'd mentioned to Debbie – the hall and lounge were affected and of course, this time we were insured! Plus, Mike was on hand to carry out the repairs! It wasn't long before I was the proud owner of a tiled hallway, and smart lounge complete with new carpet and sofa. Liam got a new laptop too!

Then came another stroke of luck. Someone told me a regulation had come in requiring banks and credit card companies to repay charges that had been unfairly raised on customers' accounts, often going back years. The PPI scandal they called it.

I had one of those cards, so I checked and it turned out mine was one of the cards affected. I filled in the various forms, not really expecting much but to my amazement and complete joy, quite a while later, a cheque for over £7,000 dropped through the letterbox.

It was like winning the lottery. A whole host of difficult bills could now be paid and there was even a little bit left over. I could almost see Grandfather beaming at me. 'Didn't I tell you it would work out fine?'

'I'll never doubt you again!' I assured him happily, even though anyone watching would have thought I was talking to an empty room.

But he wasn't finished yet. Although the unexpected windfall was like a miracle I still needed as much work as I could find. So I was delighted when one day, quite out of the blue, an email arrived from Australia. Kathleen Cox, who was from Perth, had written to say a friend had read my book, Mixed Blessings, and told her about a case I'd described, in which I'd helped the police with a murder enquiry.

I remembered it well. It involved a young man called Mark Green who'd walked out of a night club one evening and apparently vanished off the face of the earth. No one had seen him since, and he wasn't the type to just disappear, without saying a word to his family and friends.

Psychically I'd been able to reach out and contact him. It was obvious the poor lad was dead. More than that, Mark told me he'd been murdered. Although it had all happened very fast I was able to piece together the circumstances of his violent death and even tell the police when and how his body would be found. Sure enough, some time later his remains were discovered exactly as I'd predicted.

This was what had captured Kathleen's attention.

'I wondered if you could help us too?' she asked when I phoned her to discuss her problem. It turned out her niece had been found dead in tragic circumstances a few years before. The police were inclined to suspect some sort of dreadful accident but Kathleen's sister, the dead girl's mother, was convinced it was murder.

Now, sadly, the mum had passed away but Kathleen promised her dying sister she would continue the search for the truth. She wouldn't rest until she found out what really happened to her niece.

It was such a dreadful situation I wanted to help, but at that point there was no way I could afford to travel to Australia and stay there for a week or two, while I tried to make contact with the poor young girl - much as I'd like to.

'How about if I was able to organise some work for you out here?' said Kathleen. 'Then you could earn enough to pay for the flights?'

'Well that would be perfect,' I said, 'if you were able to do that.'

'Might take some time,' she said. 'Leave it with me and I'll be in touch.'

Well at least work seems to be coming my way, I thought as I put the phone down. I might never hear from Kathleen again of course but it was an encouraging sign and it lifted my spirits. And how lovely it would be to escape all the problems at home and get on with my work as usual, but thousands of miles from the stress.

It began to dawn on me that at various times in my life – usually when things were difficult, but not always - Grandfather stayed closer to me than at others. Right now I sensed him very near. Despite the fact the crisis seemed to be easing, my dear old Lined Man was still at my side. I wonder why? I thought fleetingly.

The next Sunday afternoon happened to be warm and sunny. I love the sun, and we have to make the most of it here in Wales, so as soon as lunch was cleared away I hurried out into the garden to soak up the rays. It was so relaxing just to laze back on my lounger, close my eyes and drift off, enjoying the sound of the birds singing in the trees in the paddock next door and the gentle warmth on my face. 'Bliss!' I thought.

After a while, half in a dreamy daze, I realised Grandfather was there again. 'Call this sun!' he teased, 'Now *this* is sun!' And instantly a picture of a vast open landscape formed in my mind. I was looking at miles and miles of dusty, red earth flecked with tangled thorn bushes, then huge stretches of grassland under a burning, hazy-blue sky. In the distance I could make out what looked like a group of elephants ambling slowly towards the horizon.

'Africa!' said my great, great grandfather proudly, 'Africa.'

I smiled to myself. I'd visited Africa once, years ago, as a small child. Apparently Grandfather, Ronald O. Preston, had stayed on in the country after the railway was built and some of his descendants still lived there. As a result, my father had relatives in Nairobi and one momentous holiday he took us children to visit them.

Despite some disturbing events which I wrote about in Mixed

Psychic Blessings

Blessings, I felt strangely drawn to the place. I'd love to go back and know more, I thought.

After a while I got up and went indoors to get a cold drink. All those mental pictures of the parched African bush had made me thirsty! I'd left the Sunday paper on the kitchen table and as I stood there pouring ice cold cranberry juice into a tall glass, I started idly turning the pages to see what was going on in the world.

However, what caught my eye was not the latest scandal, it was the holiday section towards the back. A package to a hotel in Mombasa, Kenya leapt out at me. I did a double take when I saw the price. It was not much over £400 per person, for an all-inclusive stay, including the flights. This was the cheapest I'd ever seen for a destination so far away – it would have cost me more for a fortnight in Llandudno! And I just happened to have a little money in the bank – not enough for Australia, but certainly sufficient for a bargain basement trip to Africa.

Instantly I wanted to go. Liam had already arranged a break with a school friend and his family, so I was free. Plus, I had the cash left over from my credit card windfall. No doubt my bank manager would have advised me to save it for future expenses, but surely I deserved a little fun after all the stress I'd been through? And of course I felt Grandfather was behind all this. Somehow or other he was engineering me to go to Africa.

I knew Peter wouldn't be able to get time off work to come with me, particularly as this was one of those last minute deals. He couldn't just drop everything. 'But if you've got some cash to spare and you want to get away, why don't you come to Dubai?' he said, when I phoned to tell him.

I sighed. Truth was, I didn't want to go to Dubai – even to see Peter – which, looking back, should have told me something. For a start, my little windfall, though enough for this super-cheap package to Mombasa would hardly cover a one-way ticket to Dubai let alone a return. How I'd get back I couldn't imagine. Then there was the fact that as Peter was working, most of my time in Dubai would be spent on my own. But more importantly, I badly wanted to go to Africa. I felt Grandfather (in my mind I call him Grandfather now – the 'great great' is too much of a mouthful!) was drawing me there and I longed to see the country that meant so much to him.

'This holiday's much cheaper than Dubai,' I said to Peter. 'I'll ask Sue to come with me.'

When the children were younger I'd often taken them on holiday without him, as Peter was working so hard to establish his business, he could seldom get away. I was quite used to making other arrangements.

Unfortunately though, as it turned out, neither Sue nor any of my friends could manage the trip either. Some had already made plans, others were broke, and the rest couldn't get the time off work.

'It's such a shame,' I said to Mike as we chatted a few nights later after the meditation class. 'It's such a brilliant deal and I'd love to go, but no one's free. Looks like I'll have to give it a miss.'

'Hang on a minute,' said Mike, 'You know I've always wanted to travel. I'll come with you if you'll put up with me!'

Mike had become a good friend over the months. While he was working on the farmhouse he'd got into the habit of dropping in after work to discuss progress and we'd end up talking for hours. He was such a good listener I'd confide my worries about Peter and the mess we were in, while Mike would tell me about his dreams of travelling the world one day. I trusted him completely. So if there was one person who'd be an ideal holiday companion, it was Mike. What's more, as he was a big, strong fella I'd feel safer with Mike by my side in a strange country, than one of my girlfriends.

So, from thinking at the beginning of the year, I'd scarcely be able to feed myself and Liam, let alone take a holiday, here I was, quite unexpectedly enjoying a safari break in Kenya.

Well, I say safari break. In fact, it was a hotel break with optional safari excursions. Sadly, these were too expensive for us to snap up when we booked so I'd imagined that regretfully, we'd have to give the big game animals a miss.

Grandfather had other ideas though.

'Wait till you get there,' Grandfather whispered in my ear, 'It will be much cheaper. Talk to the Beach Boys.'

I got the impression he was quite canny with money – or at least he tried to be - but Beach Boys? Weren't they an old pop group? What could he mean? Oh well, we'd just have to wait and see.

Anyway, our micro-budget hotel turned out to be absolutely fine and in a nice area of Mombasa. It was out a little bit on the edge of town and the beach here was quite rocky – not one of the great, white sand paradises you see in front of some hotels in the brochures. Maybe that's why it was so cheap. Whatever, it was okay with us. And as Mike was a big guy, well over 6ft tall, I always felt safe and secure with him if we happened to be walking back along the quiet streets after dark.

During the day, as we explored the pretty, modern area with its white buildings trimmed with blue, and its shady palms cooling the gardens, I couldn't help wondering what it must have looked like in Queen Victoria's time when Grandfather arrived. I'd heard that Arab dhows with great billowing sails glided across the harbour and there were narrow streets teaming with noise and colour. Back then, Mombasa was a great trading post for gold, ivory and spices and even then it was a real melting pot. People from every part of the world crammed into the port. A bit like now of course except there'd have been no sun-worshippers in skimpy bikinis draped across the pristine white sands. They'd have thought we tourists were mad!

And of course it wasn't long before I understood what Grandfather meant about the Beach Boys. Whenever we strolled on the sands outside our hotel there always seemed to be a group of young local men hanging around, waiting to offer any passing tourists sight-seeing expeditions, souvenirs to buy or personal escorts to the best restaurants in town. They were known as the Beach Boys and their prices were very, very good, they assured us.

They certainly were. Some of the other guests in the hotel were dubious but when they offered us a mini-bus safari to Tsavo National Park for a fraction of the cost we'd been quoted in the UK, I accepted immediately. Grandfather had told me to seek out the Beach Boys so I knew I could trust them. Besides, Tsavo was one of the places through which Ronald had driven the railway line and it was famous for the man-eating lions that had plagued the workers' camp. There'd even been a film about the horror, starring Michael Douglas – husband of my fellow Swansea girl, Catherine Zeta Jones. There was no way I could miss the chance to see the place for myself.

I have to admit the safari tour wasn't the most comfortable of road trips. Once out of Mombasa, our mini-bus bucketed along the rutted tarmac, bouncing from pothole to pothole through a boiling landscape of red earth, dust and dried up, bone-bleached thorn bushes. After a while we emerged into greener countryside but by this time quite a few of the passengers were desperate for a pitstop.

The driver wasn't too happy as we still had a way to go but he told us he knew a place, so to hang on a bit longer. Eventually he drew up at a huddle of buildings in a halo of welcome green, beside the highway.

We all stumbled gratefully off the bus and as we stood there blinking in the sun I felt Grandfather suddenly zoom close to my shoulder.

'Over there!' he directed. 'This is the place.'

Across the road was an inviting chalet style construction with the words 'Man Eaters Lodge' in large letters across the front. I think the driver was hoping we'd just dash in, use the conveniences and dash out again but once the passengers caught sight of the comfortable, cool interior and the well-stocked café they had other ideas. No one was leaving this lush oasis any time soon!

Within minutes everyone was sprawled around the soft seats, ordering coffee or ice cold beers, grateful for a respite from the pounding highway. But I didn't join them straight away. I'd been cramped up in a seat for long enough. I wandered around, stretching my legs while Mike sorted out our drinks, and my eye was drawn to a collection of black and white photographs on the wall. Curiously I strolled over.

'There we are,' said Grandfather in my ear.

To my amazement I was staring at a striking shot of a large tent with the flap drawn back to reveal a splendid couple sitting side by side. The woman was immaculate, in pristine, starched white blouse, ankle-length skirt and straw boater perched on her carefully upswept black hair. The man sitting beside her looked lean and tough with a dark moustache and a rifle slung casually across his knees. Between them on the floor were animal skin rugs and a splendid pair of curved horns – clearly hunting trophies. Behind was a big wooden table and what looked like a tame grey parrot hovering near the woman's shoulder.

Ronald and Florence Preston said the caption. My great, great grandfather and grandmother. My old Lined Man in his younger days.

'That was our home for five years,' said Grandfather proudly in my head, indicating the tent. 'Our camp was very close to here.'

What a fine looking couple, I thought. And how on earth did Florence manage to keep that perfect white blouse so spotless and well pressed in the middle of the bush?

'C'mon Di,' called Mike, putting some cold drinks down on the table. 'There's a talk starting.'

A talk? I moved back to the group just as a young boy came to stand in front of us. Bizarrely he began to regale the bus with a history of the Lodge and an explanation of its name.

He explained that the famous railway line was once nicknamed The Lunatic Express because it was such a crazy idea to attempt to drive a railway 660 miles across the uncharted desert, vast plains and the Great Rift Valley all the way to Lake Victoria. There were no roads or towns between there and Mombasa. It was an insane route, crawling with malaria-carrying mosquitoes, tsetse fly, scorpions and snakes, swarming with wild animals and of course terrorised by the famous man-eating lions. Thousands of men died during the construction, most from disease but a particularly unlucky few were savaged by the killer beasts.

'Here at Tsavo where a camp was set up, over a hundred railway workers were snatched from their tents and eaten by the lions,' the boy went on.

And it wasn't just the construction workers. The boy recounted the mind-boggling story of how, one night, a visiting police superintendent decided to put a stop to the killer beasts once and for all. He had his inspection carriage backed into a siding and along with two friends, sat up all night beside the open window with his gun on his knee, hoping to get a shot at the lions as they prowled round the workers' tents.

Unfortunately for him, at some point he fell asleep and during the early hours, one of the lions (a huge creature nearly ten feet long from nose to tail) forced its way through the sliding door into the carriage. It leapt onto the unlucky policeman, grabbed him by the throat, and dragged him bodily out of the carriage window into the night.

The little that was left of him was found the next morning.

It was a gruesome story and I started to feel oddly uncomfortable as I listened, yet for some reason I didn't think the sensation was caused by the fate of the poor policeman, horrible though that was. I began to fidget, but the audience was fascinated and the boy, encouraged, was just warming up.

'It was thanks to the brave Colonel Patterson,' he continued happily, 'that the reign of terror of the lions was finally brought to an end.'

Somewhere close I could feel Grandfather getting agitated. The more the boy went on about this Colonel Patterson, the angrier Grandfather became. He was getting so steamed up it was making me feel hot and irritable.

In fact, I could almost see Ronald pacing furiously up and down. In the end he was making me so uneasy I couldn't bear to hear another word. I quickly rose and, as discreetly as possible, left the group. I went back outside and climbed into the bus to wait.

I wasn't sure what the problem was but it was clear Ronald Preston hadn't been too fond of Colonel Patterson.

'About half a mile over there...' Grandfather said in my ear, indicating somewhere across the road, hidden in the undergrowth, 'is the line.'

I believe it's still possible to see the old line these days but I didn't fancy striking out on my own into the bush just then, so I decided to give it a miss on this expedition. At least Ronald seemed calmer now.

The rest of the safari was wonderful. In the National Park we saw giraffes, zebra, elephants and lions – thankfully the non-man-eating variety - and all manner of other animals and birds gathering around the water holes.

I could feel Grandfather enjoying it all, over my shoulder. In fact, he told me in advance what we were about to see and which way to look. He was in his element amongst the big game. This is where he fell in love with Africa I realised and he wanted to show me.

The rest of the holiday passed all too quickly. We went off the beaten track a bit when the Beach Boys took us to see an orphanage few tourists ever visited. The children lived in mud huts, just like you see on television but they were growing their own vegetables and showed us how they clean their teeth with little twigs taken from the eucalyptus trees that shaded the village. The method obviously worked wonders because their teeth were beautiful – perfectly white and strong. Despite everything they were such happy, smiling children even though they were barefoot and didn't own so much as a pair of shoes.

I went home determined to raise money to buy them as many little necessities as I could.

All in all it was a fascinating trip. There was only one disturbing incident. While Mike and I got on very well, we didn't always agree about everything. One morning Mike thought it would be a brilliant idea to go swimming in the sea. I wasn't so keen. The thing about the stretch of coast near our hotel was that it shelved very gently so you had to wade a long way out to find water deep enough to swim in.

Plus of course, our bay, lacking the familiar Mombasa acres of powder-puff sand to stroll on, was not so inviting to pick across.

Nevertheless, Mike was determined to give it a go so, rather reluctantly, I went with him. We started the long trek out, bare feet slapping over the sun warmed rocks. But when we finally got to the water's edge I could see the sea bed was full of rocks too, and worse, between the rocks were sea urchins with long, vicious looking black spines. I knew they were dangerous. One sting could paralyse me, I was quite sure.

I tried to stepping-stone from rock to rock but as, little by little, the water began to reach our knees it was getting more and more difficult. To be honest, I was frightened. Yet Mike, still eager for his swim, wouldn't hear of turning back. The ultimate adrenaline junkie, he just strode ahead, apparently unfazed by the thousands of toxic needles waving beneath his feet. 'Come on Di,' he encouraged. 'The water's great.'

But the waves were getting rougher, smashing against my legs and threatening to topple me off the rocks onto the unseen spines I knew lurked just below the surface.

For a moment I was so scared I could hardly move. The next second Grandfather was there.

'Stop!' he said urgently into my ear. 'Don't follow him. Get down under the water child and use your hands. Use your hands, not your feet.'

For a second I couldn't think what he meant. Then I crouched down and realised what he was getting at. By putting my face lightly into the water I could see the sea bed. The urchins showed up crystal clear and more importantly, the safe spaces between them. This meant that by keeping my face close to the surface and walking on my hands while letting my legs float out behind me, I could steer myself to safety.

It was a good idea but not as easy as it sounds. Thousands of the spiky creatures encrusted the sea bed like huge, prickly footballs. The gaps were hard to find, and as I dragged myself painfully along on my hands, the waves got rougher and rougher and kept crashing me into the rocks over and over again. My arms ached, my shoulders and hips were battered and tears were streaming down my face. I wasn't sure how much longer I could do this.

Then like a miracle, a patch of clear beach – a little sandbank – opened up in front of me and I lunged for it. Gratefully I stood upright, salty rivulets dripping off my grazed and bruised skin. Way ahead I could see Mike reach the deep water and throw himself happily into the blue.

'Come on Di! It's fine out here!' he called. 'The water's much deeper out here.'

I didn't want to be a killjoy but safe on my island, that was it.

Grandfather obviously agreed. 'Stay where you are,' he said sternly, as Mike shouted again. 'Don't move. You'll be fine.'

He needn't have worried. There was no way I was going any further and how I was going to get back didn't bear thinking about. When I looked behind me I was horrified. We'd come so far out. The beach seemed to be miles away, our hotel a little white speck in the distance. And when I turned again for a glimpse of Mike, I could hardly see him. His head kept going under and the waves were getting higher and higher. I was seriously alarmed he might drown. We'd need all of Grandfather's power to help us out of this one.

Just then, a piercing sound floated over the crashing waves.

'Diane! Missus!'

I looked round. One of the Beach Boys was running towards me from the direction of the hotel, waving his arms.

'No, missus. Stop!'

I was already stopped, so I stayed where I was and stared at him.

'Stay there Diane! Don't move.'

He was still waving his arms and as he drew closer I could see he was waving a pair of jelly shoes.

'You must put them on!' he puffed when he finally splashed up to me. 'You're gonna need these to get back! It's not safe. You should never have come out here on your own. People have died out here. There are electric jellyfish everywhere, not just sea urchins.'

I didn't need telling twice. Gratefully I tugged on a pair of shoes.

'Thank you so much!' I said.

We looked round for Mike. Far away I could see his head bobbing under the waves, then reappearing a little further off.

He didn't seem to be getting very far but gradually, painfully I realised he was getting closer.

It seemed to take ages, but eventually he staggered out of the ocean and lurched onto the sandbank beside us. He looked exhausted.

'Thank God you didn't come in Di,' he said. 'I only just made it. There was such a powerful undertow I nearly went under so many times.'

And Mike was fit. Mike climbed mountains, he did a lot of surfing and he was a strong swimmer. If *he* barely got back in one piece, I'd have stood no chance.

Shaking his head at such foolishness the Beach Boy led us back via some safer route through the rocks that only the locals knew.

Thank goodness for the Lined Man and his warning I thought as we threaded our way back to the hotel – Grandfather had saved me again.

Three

Fire. There was fire all around me. Hideous orange flames leaping up everywhere I looked, and I seemed to be in some sort of sealed box that was rapidly filling with smoke. I couldn't get out!

Panic rising, I forced my mind to draw back from the horrifying scene. It wasn't a sealed box, I could see now. I was in a car. Heat was scorching my face and the smoke was choking my throat. I tried to claw at the window but it wouldn't open properly and I couldn't seem to move from the seat. The car was getting hotter and hotter…

'I'm boiling!' a voice cried out in my mind.

It was too much. I wrenched my attention away from the nightmare situation and back to the present. Here I was standing in the car park of a perfectly ordinary little retail park in Perth, Australia. Perfectly ordinary shoppers were coming and going from their cars and stashing their purchases in various boots. A safer, more mundane setting would be hard to imagine. Yet incredibly, a few years before, this innocuous car park was the scene of a dreadful tragedy.

A few of the shoppers glanced curiously my way and who could blame them? Here I was, a grown woman, standing in the middle of an empty bay, clutching a photograph, a necklace and a large toy rabbit.

How could they have known these items weren't mine? They belonged to the late Debbie Anderson and their vibrations were helping me make contact with their former owner. Poor Debbie was a young English student who'd only arrived in Australia a few months before. She'd been found dead in a burned-out car on this very spot a decade earlier.

Kathleen Cox, the woman who'd contacted me about visiting Australia to try to find out what had happened to her niece, was standing nearby, along with a couple of intrigued newspaper reporters. We must have looked an odd group.

'He was a savage!' Debbie said suddenly in my ear. 'A total savage.'

And as my attention switched back to the tragedy, the flames disappeared and Debbie showed me instead a scruffy young man with dark skin, dressed in jeans, and a shabby brown tee shirt with some sort of fish design on the front. An overpowering smell of sweat and chewing tobacco clung to this figure, and when he leered through the car window at Debbie you could see tobacco stains yellowing his big square teeth. He was tugging at the door handle which Debbie hadn't bothered to lock and as I watched, the door suddenly swung open and he slid inside.

'It wasn't an accident!' I said to Kathleen. 'Debbie was murdered.'

'We knew it! We knew it!' said Kathleen, a mix of triumph and relief in her voice. Apparently with no witnesses and nothing else to go on, the police had suggested Debbie might have fallen asleep in the car with a cigarette in her hand and accidentally set fire to herself. It could even have been suicide.

'Her mother never believed that,' said Kathleen, 'and neither did I.' They'd been trying ever since to get justice for Debbie but if no one even knew if a crime had been committed, it was proving impossible.

I was so glad Kathleen had been able to organise this visit for me. Debbie was sick of her family being told she was responsible for her own death. She wanted people to know the truth and I've no doubt she helped her aunt make the arrangements to raise the necessary funds.

As luck (or Debbie and her late mum working from the other side) would have it, Kathleen managed to book the Octagon

Theatre on the University of Western Australia's campus for my demonstration, and by working very hard, she was able to sell enough tickets to pay for my airfare to Perth.

I'd never been to Australia before so even though it was a very long flight, it was wonderful to have the opportunity to visit. Perth turned out to be a lovely city. The residential areas were spacious and tree-lined with big houses set back from the road, and when we drove along the beautiful waterfront, I was fascinated to notice the pedestrian paths were dotted with barbeque points and outdoor gym equipment for passers-by to use as they pleased. What a great idea I thought. We could do with some of that in Swansea!

The theatre appearance had been booked for the beginning of my trip, soon after I arrived and before my investigation into Debbie's death so it was number one on my itinerary. True, I was a bit jet-lagged from the long flight of course, but I wasn't too fazed, even though I have to admit, I do still get nervous in front of an audience. Everyone thinks doing shows gets easier the more you do but, strangely enough it doesn't. Not for me anyway. My stomach still churns in the hours before I step on stage and I can feel quite sick before I walk out in front of all those people, no matter how many shows I do. Still, compared to my very first attempt a few years before, I felt like an old pro.

I will never ever forget my very first stage show at the tiny little theatre in Llanelli, not far from my home. What a struggle that had been!

It came about just after I'd won Britain's Psychic Challenge. Several demanding and exciting weeks of working with the TV crew and the other impressive psychics had come to an end, and the completion of the challenge left me feeling slightly flat. It was a bit of an anti-climax. I sensed the spirit world didn't intend for me to stop here. I was to use my award as a stepping-stone rather than an end in itself. I got the very strong feeling I was being directed to do something new with my gift – trouble was, my guides weren't making it clear to me exactly what.

'Why don't you do a theatre show?' suggested my sister Debbie, when I explained my dilemma. 'Plenty of other psychics do.'

True, I'd always dreamed of appearing on stage one day, but not yet! I didn't feel ready so it was an alarming idea. However, the more I mulled it over, the more I realised it was probably just the new challenge I needed. I'll start very small, I thought to myself, as a sort of compromise. I'll go down to that little theatre I'd noticed, passing through Llanelli, and see what they say.

Llanelli is a small town on the Loughor estuary, close to the sea and not far from Swansea. It was the perfect location. As easy for me to reach as Swansea, though nowhere near as intimidating as the big bustling city. I wasn't ready to take on the bright lights just yet! I wasn't even sure how you go about organising a show, but when I phoned the theatre they told me to come down and discuss my plan with a gentleman called Erwin.

As soon as I found the address I knew this theatre would be a good place to work in. The building was quite old fashioned, but in a good way. As I pushed open the heavy glass door it was like stepping back in time. Everywhere I looked I could see plush red and velvet. A crimson carpeted staircase curved gracefully up to the balcony and the delicious smell of old wood mingled with the scent of popcorn and fried onions, hung in the air – nectar as far as I'm concerned! It took me right back to when I was a child queuing up for the cinema full of anticipation and longing for a hot dog: I loved it.

Then I noticed, just inside the foyer a smartly dressed man sitting in a grand scarlet armchair in front of a small polished table, was eyeing me suspiciously.

As I met his gaze, he immediately fired a stream of incomprehensible Welsh in my direction.

'I'm sorry,' I said when he paused, obviously expecting me to answer some question that to me was completely unintelligible. 'I can only understand a very little Welsh. I certainly can't speak it.'

He seemed disappointed and maybe a tad disapproving. This had to be Erwin. I thought to myself. Not a great start.

'So you're not Welsh then?' he said, reverting to English.

'Well, yes I am,' I said. 'In fact I grew up in Swansea and these days I only live about twenty minutes from here.' I told him where I was from and it turned out he knew the village.

This seemed to soften him a bit but not a lot!

'So tell me about yourself,' he went on abruptly. 'Why do you want to work in this theatre? So you've done a bit of TV – what else?'

'I've done some radio too,' I said and explained about the late night slot I often did on a local radio station in Swansea.

'Never heard of it,' said Erwin. I could have cried. He certainly wasn't making it easy for me. 'What makes you think you can fill a whole theatre? Have you got a company, or is it just little you?'

The way he said 'little you' sounded a bit scornful to me and my confidence slumped even lower. Goodness this is just like a job interview, I thought, and it's not going well! I felt like turning round and rushing home. Bet my great great grandfather and the other spirits were pushing me on.

'As a matter of fact, I have got a company,' I said defiantly. 'It's called Psychic Productions.'

I don't know whether Erwin meant a theatre company, the sort of thing that puts on plays and pantomimes but as far as I was concerned a company's a company and I could truthfully say I had one – just about! Only one week before, my dear old father-in-law Harry, who knew about these things, said to me, 'Why don't you have your own limited company Diane, now you've won Psychic Challenge? It might make things easier for you. I'll set it up for you if you like.'

And bless him, he did.

Erwin seemed to soften a bit more at the mention of my company. The tone of his voice changed slightly.

'Hmm. And you think you can fill this theatre?'

'I know we can,' I bluffed.

'Well you've got to be sure,' he said.

'I'm absolutely sure,' I said, and before I knew it I heard myself adding, 'that I can fill it - for two nights!' I stopped, shocked at the words that had popped out of my mouth. Two nights? Where did that come from?

Erwin seemed appalled. 'What are you saying? You want to work here for two nights running? D'you know how many seats this theatre holds?'

'Yes!' I said. I reckoned it was about 500. 'And yes. I want two nights.'

'Don't you think you're being a bit ridiculous Diane?' he scoffed.

'No,' I blustered, though inwardly I agreed with him. It was crazy. How could I possibly fill a 500 seat theatre two nights running? Even so, inside my head a powerful voice was saying, 'You'll do it Diane. We'll help you.'

'It won't be ridiculous,' I insisted recklessly to Erwin. 'In fact it'll be a sell out!'

He shook his head, resignedly. He clearly didn't believe me, but he couldn't be bothered to argue any more. 'Well if you want to risk it. It's your reputation at stake. I won't stand in your way.'

I breathed a sigh of relief. I'd had no idea it would be so difficult even to get a theatre, let alone put on a show, but at least now the first hurdle was over.

Debbie and I went into a blur of activity. We had some posters and flyers printed and a bunch of friends, along with our cousins and our mum kindly distributed them for us.

Then Debbie and I hit town to find something suitable for me to wear. We discovered a funny little shop in Swansea that sold designer clothes at amazingly cheap prices. It was very cluttered inside, with tightly packed racks everywhere you looked and dressing rooms adorned with curtains so skimpy they didn't quite close. Yet amongst the chaos my hands fell on two lovely suits – one in red silk, the other in turquoise and as I was trying them on, with Debbie doing her best to hold the curtains of my cubicle together, we heard another customer come into the shop. All at once, a familiar husky voice came floating over the crammed hangers as the newcomer chatted to the assistant.

I peered out through the gap above Debbie's hands. 'Debbie look!' I whispered. We both stuck our heads out. It was the amazing Bonnie Tyler, the legendary singer. I knew she lived in Swansea and it looked as if she might buy her stage clothes here too. Well if it's good enough for Bonnie Tyler, I thought, it's certainly good enough for me!

My spirit friends kept their word. Astonishingly, all our tickets were sold for both shows, just as I'd predicted and the opening night raced round far too quickly.

I was so nervous beforehand I could hardly string two words together – except of course when I was telling Debbie, 'I can't do it Debbie. It's no good: I can't go on.'

'Yes of course you can,' she insisted. She wouldn't hear of me making an excuse to dash home. Instead she steered me to the theatre bar and ordered a vodka. And as I stood there, knees knocking, vodka in one hand and Debbie's hand squeezed tightly in the other I looked round and saw the late, great medium Doris Stokes standing by my side.

I often explain to people that we can't just call up any celebrity or famous person in spirit that we fancy having a chat to because we would have loved to speak to them in life but never got the chance. It doesn't work like that. You have to be connected to the spirit in some way in order for them to come to talk to you. But as it happened, although I'd never met Doris while she was on earth, I'd become connected to her a few years back through her ghostwriter Linda Dearsley. I met Linda, and her daughter, Emma, while I was filming Psychic Challenge. We'd become friends and she went on to help me with my first book Mixed Blessings.

Doris always seemed to be close to Linda. When we were working together on the book I'd often see Doris sitting beside her, smiling away as we chatted, clearly taking an interest in the whole procedure. And now here she was again, right in the bar with Debbie and me!

She leaned forward, touched my arm in a comforting way and into my mind came a soothing voice.

'I used to do shows too Diane,' she said, 'and just like you I used to be so nervous. But we have to trust. We have to let people know that we survive, we live on. I'll be here to help you. I'll be by your side right through the show – never forget that. And if you can't hear the voices, just ask for Doris in your mind and I'll get them to slow down and speak clearly for you to hear.'

She used to do shows. I happened to know for a fact from Linda that Doris had appeared at the London Palladium and the Sydney Opera House, amongst other prestigious venues. The tiny theatre of Llanelli hardly compared, yet here she was offering to help.

All at once a great calmness seemed to slip over me and sink down through my body from the top of my head and right on to my feet. Doris disappeared but I knew it was going to be alright.

I turned to Debbie. 'It's okay,' I said. 'I'm ready now. Let's go.'

We put our glasses back on the bar and headed backstage.

Standing in the wings together, we heard my pre-recorded music start to play, then as Debbie watched, I walked out onto the stage. The curtains opened and suddenly I was blinded by lights – which suited me because I couldn't see the scary sight of all those hundreds of upturned faces out there, looking at me. I could feel them though.

Quickly, before I could change my mind I started to introduce myself and then somehow, I was off. Words came tumbling out of my mouth without my having to think about them and then the spirit voices arrived. The lights were turned down now, so I could see the audience, but I no longer minded those rows and rows of faces.

'You!' I said, pointing to a lady half way back. 'I've got a message for you.'

The woman shrieked, 'I don't believe in all this! I only came to see the way you worked.'

'Tell her she was in the dentist's today,' said a voice into my ear.

'So, you've been to the dentist today!' I told her.

Her mouth fell open and she straightened abruptly in her seat. 'Yes I have,' she agreed, 'In fact I only got out of there about 5.00 this afternoon. How in the world do you know that?'

'Well your mother just told me she came to the dentist with you,' I explained.

'And she keeps giving me the name Marian.'

Tears started to roll down the woman's face. 'That's my mother's name,' she said. 'She only passed away four weeks ago.'

'Well she came to the dentist with you today and she wanted you to come here tonight.'

'It should have been my friend who came,' said the woman,

'but she hurt her ankle and couldn't walk, so she gave me the ticket so as not to waste it.'

Marian drew back and another voice came in, a male voice this time. 'And please tell your friend,' I went on slowly, 'that her dad Bryn wants her to know he loves her and he says to tell the grandchildren they're all looked after spiritually.' A quick vision of two young twin boys flashed into my mind, 'And the little boys, the twins, are really cute.'

The woman was almost falling off her seat by now. 'That's right Diane. She does have twin boys. Thank you so much. I'm so glad I came…'

That was the first message of the night and after that I was on a roll. Information kept pouring out and I found myself drawn to person after person.

'I need to come to you!' I said at one point, indicating a very tall gentleman near the front with vivid orange hair. 'I can see a beautiful dog beside you. Looks like a German Shepherd to me.'

At that the poor man began to cry.

'Oh… and what an unusual name to call your dog!' I added, 'I'm sure they said his name is Jeremy!'

The man started to laugh through his tears and the rest of the audience laughed with him. 'That's right,' he said. 'I named him after my long lost brother! Thank you again Diane. I saw you on that Channel 5 show and I was impressed.'

'Well your brother Jeremy and your dog Jeremy are always with you,' I said, 'and your brother's got hair just like yours.' I paused as a picture of a building surrounded by countryside flashed into my mind, 'Now he's showing me a farmhouse you used to visit together when you were kids.'

'That'll be our Grandma's place up in England,' said the man. 'We used to go there a lot.'

At once the picture changed and I was looking at two small

boys in shorts and wellies, giggling as they fiddled about with a big old-fashioned tractor in the farmyard.

'That tractor!' said the man, as I described what I was seeing. 'I haven't thought about that for years. But you're right. It had been standing there for about 10 years and we thought we could fix it. We couldn't but we had a good laugh trying!'

And so it went on. By the time the show finished I felt like I was flying. Exhausted but exhilarated at the same time. As I walked off the stage, deafening applause was bouncing round the walls and I noticed Doris walking beside me. She was wearing an elegant long blue dress that swished and sparkled in the lights as she moved. As I registered her appearance, she saw and smiled at me then she glanced down at my feet.

'You should make sure you wear comfortable shoes Diane,' she said. 'I know what it's like. I used to do shows just like you and you need to look after your feet.'

Curiously I looked at her own feet. Sparkly shoes that matched her dress peeped out beneath the hem at every step, but sure enough, they were totally flat. Mine on the other hand had mile high heels. I smiled to myself. She was quite right. After a couple of hours standing on stage in those shoes, my feet were killing me!

All in all it was a fantastic start to theatre demonstrations, and I was to go on to do many more, so apart from my usual nerves, the Octagon in Perth was nowhere near as scary!

The University of Western Australia campus turned out to be a spacious, airy place with clusters of vaguely Italianate looking buildings and more of those tall, graceful trees I seemed to see all over Perth. *Lucky students*, I couldn't help thinking as Kathleen took me inside.

The actual demonstration passed in a blur and I remembered little of it afterwards but oddly enough, at the end, a young woman came up to me out of the audience.

'I have to tell you Diane, I'm from Wales too,' she said, 'and I went to your old school! We were in different years though, so we never met. My mum came to see you a while back in Swansea and you told her I was going to be a hairdresser. So guess what I'm doing now?'

'You're a hairdresser!' I laughed because I could see instantly that she was.

'Right!' she agreed and she started laughing too. Talk about a small world!

But of course, the main reason for my visit was to try to find out what happened to Kathleen's niece. A couple of days later Kathleen picked me up in her car, with her sweet little whippet dog in the back and we drove out to the small shopping centre where Debbie's body had been discovered.

I hung onto the personal items of Debbie's that Kathleen had found for me, and wandered slowly back and forth around the tarmac area where the burned out car had been found. I could see the low rise retail units all around, reassuringly mundane and safe looking, yet I could feel how different it must have been late at night when that white car had rolled to a stop in this very bay and parked for the last time. Everything was closed. There was no one about. The whole place was dark and deserted. Debbie must have felt so lonely.

'I told them I was going to the zoo,' Debbie said suddenly in my ear. 'But I wasn't.'

'Yes that's right,' said Kathleen. 'She borrowed her dad's partner's car to go to the zoo but we believe she never got there.'

It seemed Debbie had two relationships at the time, one of them with an older man who was possibly married, which is perhaps why he hadn't come forward.

'We were going to meet,' Debbie told me, 'but then this... savage... jumped in the car.'

I got the impression of the car, now stationary, and a big

struggle going on. Debbie was fighting and scratching. She put up a huge fight. The attacker must have ended up with wounds to the left side of his face. But then she was head butted, strong hands gripped her round the throat and she fell unconscious.

I was sure the man raped her, then set fire to the car and walked away. Horrifyingly, at some point, Debbie must have come to, just in time to see him sauntering off because she showed me a mind picture of the silhouette of a man disappearing on foot towards the exit, as flames roared around the vehicle.

'The police were under-manned,' Debbie went on. 'They didn't catch him. But someone knows this man. Someone will come forward.'

I tried to focus on the attacker in case I could discover any more scraps of information that might help the police. I got the strong impression he'd decided to rape Debbie the moment he managed to get inside the car. He maybe didn't expect to gain access. When unexpectedly he did, he couldn't believe his luck.

This man was something of a drifter. He had a terrible temper and I felt he'd committed crimes before and served time in prison. Now he wanted to travel but couldn't because there was some problem over his papers. I sensed he came from a big family. He had several brothers but didn't get on with them.

A glimpse of his father flitted into my mind. He was an older man who wore his hair in a pony-tail and he seemed to do outdoor work of some kind – he was probably a gardener because I got a glimpse of him surrounded by plants.

Then another image appeared. It was the scruffy attacker again, only this time he had a nasty smirk on his face and he was holding a skirt. A skirt with a big rip in it.

'He's got Debbie's skirt!' I said. 'He's kept it as a souvenir.'

'I wanted to open my own restaurant one day you know,' said Debbie's voice, as she moved close again. 'I would have done too.'

'Yes, that was her dream,' said Kathleen. 'She was loving her course. She had everything to live for.'

It was so sad. Debbie couldn't tell us any more, but hopefully we'd come up with a few details that would be useful to the police. I found out later they'd been puzzled about the unusual movements of the borrowed car. It had been recorded driving 800 kilometres that day, way out of Perth and then back again.

Perhaps Debbie's abductor had forced her to drive and drive before bringing her back to Perth, under cover of darkness, to destroy the evidence.

But as Debbie said. *Somebody* must be saying to themselves, 'I know this man'.

One day they will come forward.

I do hope so anyway.

Four

It was around 8.00pm when I heard the knock on the door. Liam and I exchanged glances. We weren't expecting any visitors and it was dark outside. Here we were, rattling around in this big house on our own. I'm not the nervous type – not really – but even so, sometimes it was a bit worrying being here on my own in this quiet country lane, with just a schoolboy and my tiny dog Rocky, to ward off burglars.

Before I could stop him, Liam jumped up. 'I'll go!'

'Any of your mates coming round?' I asked.

'Don't think so...' called Liam over his shoulder as he trotted away, then he was gone.

But a few seconds later there came a big shout. 'Mum it's the police!'

My stomach turned over. Even when you're psychic, you can't help fearing the worst when the police turn up unexpectedly.

Oh my goodness. I hope nobody's hurt, I thought. And I hope this has nothing to do with Peter and the business problems!

I hurried to the door. There on the step were two police officers in full uniform. One was tall, with a long, lean face, the other shorter and rather round. Behind them, in the lane, I could see their police car with the blue light on the top. What would the neighbours make of that? I wondered.

'Are you Mrs Diane Lazarus?' asked the policeman.

'Yes,' I said.

'I understand you have some information for us,' said the thin one. 'About a man called Ian Jones.'

Ah, now I understood. That afternoon I'd discovered I'd accidentally brought the office mobile home with me – something I never normally do - and while I was cooking tea, it started buzzing like crazy.

It was a text. 'Please help me,' I read, 'I need your help urgently Diane. My partner's gone missing and I know you're the only person that can help. I've been in touch with the police and I've told them I'm going to contact you because I know you're really good at finding people.'

Well, I thought as I turned off the stove. This was obviously meant to be. I've never brought the office phone home before. I'm clearly meant to speak to this woman.

Ever since I won Britain's Psychic Challenge I'd been getting calls from all over the world from people who hoped I could find their various missing loved ones from vanished children and partners to beloved cats, dogs and even cherished pieces of jewellery. These people had obviously heard about a couple of the psychic challenges shown in the TV series that involved finding, first, a man camouflaged and hidden in woodland, and later a boy concealed in miles of sand dunes. These particular challenges suited me very well and I'd found both volunteers in record time. So now I seemed to have become the 'go-to' woman when finding skills were required.

I try to help in as many cases as I can, though sometimes I know the hopeful enquirers won't want to hear what I have to tell them. So now, I quickly called the woman back. It turned out her name was Sarah and she explained she and her partner had been having some difficulties. Finally, there was a small argument and Ian walked out. Sarah didn't think it was a serious disagreement but he hadn't returned. Now she was frantic with worry.

'Well look, send me his photograph,' I said as soothingly as I could, 'and I'll see if I can pick anything up.'

A few minutes later a picture of a serious-looking young man with troubled eyes pinged into my inbox. Even as I took in his features, a vision started appearing in my head. I could see a small silver car driving around and Ian was at the wheel. Then the car stopped and I watched him climb out and walk into a shop to buy a packet of cigarettes and a bottle of cider. Soon the car was moving off again but I could make out some strange stuff in the back. I wasn't sure what it was but there seemed to be some sort of hosepipe. Then the car pulled up again. It had come to a stop in a quiet patch of waste ground with a group of run-down buildings, possibly garages nearby. I got the feeling it wasn't far from his home and I didn't like what I was seeing. I had a bad feeling about this.

Quickly I called Sarah back. 'Do you have a small silver car?' I asked.

'Yes,' she said eagerly. 'So you've seen him in the car have you?'

'Get the police to contact me,' I said. 'Maybe they'll recognise my description of the place where he's parked.'

I suppose I imagined I'd get a phone call the next morning perhaps, or maybe the police would scoff at the idea of speaking to a psychic and refuse to contact me at all, so I was pretty astonished when the two officers actually turned up at my door within the hour. They must have been very worried about poor Mr Jones.

'You'd better come in,' I told them. 'We'll go into my study.'

The tall officer followed me respectfully. 'I've heard a lot about you Diane,' he said. 'Some of my family have been to you for readings and given good reports, so I reckon you're the real deal.'

His companion was more sceptical. He rolled his eyes behind his colleague's back. 'If you could do what you say you do, you'd know the lottery numbers wouldn't you?' he said with a smirk. 'So how about it then? What are the numbers for this weekend?'

I ignored him and sat down.

'Look,' I said to the nice one. 'I need you to tell Sarah it's not good news. I can't tell her. I hate to be the bearer of bad tidings.'

'What d'you mean by that?' snapped Mr Sceptical.

I looked at the vision that was unfolding again in my mind's eye. The events had moved on from my last glimpse.

'I can see him pulled up in his car,' I said, 'he's got himself a bottle of cider and a pack of cigarettes. Now he's slumped on the wheel of his car and it looks to me as if he's drunk all the cider, smoked all the cigarettes and he's put a hose pipe through a little gap in the window.'

'So you actually think he's dead do you Diane?' the tall one asked.

'I'm afraid I do,' I said. 'Trouble is I can't figure out exactly where he is. It's waste ground near to his house and there are some old garages there. He was planning to kill himself when he left the house, that's why he had the hosepipe in his car. He's succeeded. I don't feel you're going to get to him in time: that's the sad thing. I don't feel you're going to find him tonight. I think he was already unconscious by the time you got here.'

Mr Sceptical glared at me. Half disbelieving, half scared. 'How d'you know these things? Who told you?'

'I'm psychic,' I explained patiently. 'That's why I know. I have visions. I had a vision of him dead.'

'Well what are we gonna do about it?'

'Keep looking I suppose,' I said, 'but you won't find him till tomorrow.'

'Well we've got people out looking for him right now,' he said defiantly, 'I expect we'll find him soon.'

'You won't,' I repeated. 'It'll be tomorrow.'

And off they went, with mixed feelings I expect.

That night it was difficult to sleep. If only I'd been able to find the poor man's exact location, I kept thinking as I tossed and turned. If only they'd called me earlier. Though deep down I knew nothing would have prevented this tragedy. The spirit world works in mysterious ways. For whatever reason, it was Ian's time to move on.

The next morning the tall policeman phoned. He sounded bemused.

'Diane, I have to say you're pretty amazing!' he said. 'We've found him, exactly as you said. There were cigarettes on his passenger seat with an empty flagon of cider next to them, and the pipe was going into his car through the window, just like you said. And guess what? The car was at the side of a garage about a mile from his house.'

They thanked me for my help and they also broke the devastating news to Sarah, for which I was very grateful. I loathe having to tell people these awful things. It's such a dreadful task. Yet despite her grief I think Sarah understood. She even sent me a sweet text later, thanking me for my input.

It was coming up to Christmas again by now. I could hardly believe it was over a year since Peter left. We'd been apart all this time, doing our best to keep our marriage alive via Skype – which wasn't easy. We weren't even going to be able to spend the holidays together this year. I'd had to accept every job going to help pay the mortgage, and there was no way I could take several weeks off for a trip to Dubai. At his end, Peter said he couldn't afford to be away from his job for more than a couple of days either, and he didn't have the funds for the sky high prices for Christmas flights home. Christmas really is the worst time to fly I reckon, but it meant it was going to be difficult to summon up much festive spirit.

In the meantime though, I was busy changing offices. It was still awkward being based in the village and feeling disapproving eyes following me every day as I scuttled to and fro. Maybe I was being over-sensitive or maybe it was my imagination but I felt so many people in the area were still angry over the collapse of Peter's business, that just the sight of me reminded them of their losses. I could feel little poisonous glances spike into my back wherever I went and conversations tended to fall silent as I passed, only to resume when I'd gone by. Of course they may not have been talking about me. But it felt as if they were – and not in a good way.

What's more, reasonably priced though my little premises were, the rent was still higher than I could afford. I spent hours going over every detail of my budget, looking for ways to economise, and a cheaper office would help enormously. And if it was in a place where no one knew me or my husband, what a bonus that would be! But it seemed impossible.

'Swansea!' said a voice in my head one day as I agonised over my latest depressing bank statement.

Swansea? I questioned. Surely not a good idea. Surely a bigger town would have bigger rents to match?

But: 'Swansea,' repeated the voice.

I shrugged. Oh well. We'll see what happens. I didn't think much more of it at the time. Yet a few days later, as I was driving towards the town for my weekly anonymous grocery shopping, I noticed a newish retail mall on the edge of the built-up area, with a sign outside offering units to rent.

It seemed a longshot but the next day I phoned and I ended up meeting the owner who was a surprisingly down to earth, friendly man, named Mark. To look at him, with his casual clothes and unassuming manner, you'd never have thought he owned the whole place, but he did. He showed me around, himself, and offered me a perfect little space, in a quiet corner of the building at a rent even more reasonable than my original office.

I was impressed. There was a smart, carpeted entrance, plenty of places to park and it was an easy drive from home.

Before long I was happily settled in and what a relief it was not to have to run the gauntlet of Peter's disappointed ex-employees. Here, I was just another face in the crowd. The slate was wiped clean and I didn't have to feel guilty for anything.

Mark took to dropping by when he was passing for a quick reading, and we became good friends. He only half believed in my work, I suspect but he was intrigued to hear what I'd say next and we always ended up having a laugh. Sadly, I picked up that he didn't have very long to live but I knew he didn't want to be told about such things, maybe he even sensed it himself, so we kept our conversations light.

In the end, though I'd been dreading it, Christmas turned out to be a happy time. Lisa was able to get home from Dubai. Liam was already here of course. Then Mum, and her partner Don joined us; old family friend Beryl, who was like a grandma to me piled in as well, with her husband Peter; and one of Lisa's gay friends, Sofia, dropped by too. I was Cook, Cleaner and general hostess of course, but that was fine by me. We were a merry crowd round the dinner table. Mum, who's got a wicked sense of humour and has a wonderful knack for remembering jokes, kept us practically choking with laughter over our turkey as we ate, while Sofia, always hysterically funny at the best of times, got more and more outrageous as the day wore on. We pulled crackers and tried to keep our silly paper hats in place, over slippery heads. It turned out to be a wonderful Christmas.

Though it was poignant too, because as I looked across at Beryl, with her big blue eyes, shiny silver hair and stylish lemon cardigan, I had the overwhelming feeling this would be her last Christmas.

Beryl had been suffering from breast cancer. She'd endured quite a bit of chemotherapy over the past months and I'd been going over every week to her bungalow in Carmarthen to give her healing. We'd become very close during those sessions. Beryl was a great listener and even though I was the one doing the healing, I soon found myself confiding all my troubles over Peter and our nightmare finances. I came to think of her almost as the grandma I never had.

Right now it was so good to see her looking healthy and happy and free from pain. She was certain she was in remission. Yet I had a horrible feeling the cancer was going to return with a vengeance next year. Well, if this was to be her last Christmas, I was determined she'd enjoy it to the full.

'Come on then, Mum,' I prompted, as our brilliant entertainer paused to take a sip of her drink. 'Tell Beryl that one you were telling me the other day about the man who lost his car in the supermarket car park!' And soon the whole table was crying with laughter again.

I'd even managed a long chat with Peter on Skype Christmas morning too, which cheered me up.

Peter seemed well and content enough, though like me, he said he was finding it difficult being so far apart. All we could do, we reassured each other, was keep working as hard as we could and little by little we'd restore our finances, and finally have more options for the future.

At other times though, we ended up arguing. It was such an open-ended arrangement. Liam was doing well at school and had no wish to live in Dubai full time. I couldn't leave Liam and I didn't want to leave my beloved mum either. Mum was not getting any younger and she was my rock. I was so glad she was close by in Swansea. She often came to the office with me and acted as my assistant, answering the phone while I was doing readings and putting clients at ease while they waited. She enjoyed being busy and I loved having her near.

It was a perfect arrangement. I hated the idea of giving it all up and heading for Dubai but it was plain Peter had no intention of coming back. Maybe divorce was the only answer. Peter wouldn't hear of it though. We'd work it out somehow, he assured me.

In the end though, not long into the New Year, Peter said the other words I'd been anticipating for a long time.

'Diane, I think we'll have to sell the house.'

Deep down, I knew he was right. As we were struggling to make ends meet, it was madness to try to hang onto this big house – particularly with only Liam and I currently rattling around in it, with no knowing when, or even *if*, Peter would ever come back to live there. Plus of course, at the back of my mind, even though I pretended not to, I did know the answer to that question. Peter was never going to live in this house again. His future lay in Dubai. I'd seen it with my own eyes during that reading he was so desperate for me to do. So what was the point of half killing myself with work to try to pay for a place that would never be our family home again?

Despite everything, it made me sad to think of parting with the place. It had been my dream house and I'd been so thrilled and amazed at our good fortune when we were able to buy it. So ecstatic when we moved in. It was such a happy time in our marriage.

Set back from the road, not far from our farmhouse I used to pass by the imposing building every evening when I walked the beloved little dog I had then – a cheeky Scottie dog, black as a South Wales coal mine, called Millie.

As we came to my favourite house, I'd slow down and saunter past, letting Millie snuffle around the bushes to her heart's content while I discreetly soaked up every detail of the building. The house was fairly new, double fronted with a grand front door which overlooked a spacious gravel area inside the gate, just crying out for a pond and a little fountain to bring it to life.

Out the back I'd heard there was a large patio complete with swimming pool. Imagine living there, I used to think. What wonderful summers you could enjoy. You'd never need to go on holiday!

My daydreaming walks must have gone on for months, if not years. Then one evening, as I dawdled by, I was amazed to spot a 'For Sale' sign in the garden. Instantly, I could picture us living there. I could see myself driving up to that fancy front door, unloading a pile of shopping and carrying it inside.

It seemed impossible, but my instincts were never wrong. I raced home to Peter.

'Peter!' I called as I burst in. 'Peter, my dream house is up for sale! Is there any way we could buy it, d'you think?'

Peter laughed. 'Diane you've not even seen the inside!'

'I know!' I giggled, 'But I know I'll love it!'

He shook his head in mock resignation but all the same, the next day he made some enquiries, juggled some finances and eventually discovered we could arrange the necessary mortgage.

Just as I expected, I loved the house the moment I walked in the door. Okay, so some of the carpets and furnishing were not my style, but we could change them when we could afford it. There was a spacious hall, a broad, generous staircase leading to a galleried landing, a large, sunny sitting room and a bright kitchen you could fit a table in. Out the back, I spied the fabled swimming pool, gleaming, luscious and turquoise as an exotic jewel, in the centre of the paved patio.

Unfortunately, there was also a sad story attached to the house. The builder had built it for himself. It was his dream home too. He'd lived there contentedly for some time until he'd fallen ill and eventually passed away.

As we walked into his old study I saw oxygen masks and medical paraphernalia still spread forlornly across the desk, and then I caught a glimpse of the man himself, sitting in the chair. As if he felt my eyes on him, he suddenly swivelled round to face me. 'Brain tumour,' he said, pointing to his head, and I could see a little shaved area around his ear. 'Thing is, I'd like you to have the house, with my blessing. My partner wants to keep it and stay on here but I'd like it sold. I want the money shared among my children.'

Fortunately, Peter liked the place as much as I did and was quite happy to make an offer. So the old builder got his wish. Everything fell rapidly into place. We were able to buy his lovely house, hopefully his children benefited from a very welcome chunk of cash, and for a while, until the recession hit and torpedoed Peter's business, the Lazarus family lived there very happily. Now though, I had to face the fact that it was over. The house would have to be sold. But where will I live? I wondered vaguely. We still had the farmhouse but there was a tenant in residence.

A tiny sound behind me interrupted my thoughts. I glanced round and was startled to see, there in the middle of the kitchen a young man in soldier's uniform was standing looking at me. He gestured towards his clothes and I saw they were soaking wet and stuck to his body. There was water dripping from his hair too. Then, with a quick shake of his head, his hair was dry again and his uniform pristine and unblemished. He grinned and I recognised him.

'Blake!' I said. 'I remember you.'

He nodded, the light catching his strawberry blonde hair. Then he held up his hand and instantly I saw a pretty little town, of picture-postcard wooden chalets, snow cushioning their rooftops, and towering white mountains behind.

I recognised it immediately. 'Chamonix,' I said.

'I always wanted to live there,' said Blake.

'And I'd love to go back there,' I said. It was true. I'd fallen in love with the place when I visited a few years before, while trying to find out what had happened to Blake, who'd gone missing from the town. 'But it wouldn't be practical for me to move there just now, if that's what you mean.'

Blake smiled again. 'Nice idea though,' he said. 'Think about it. I never got the chance but maybe one day you will.' And he faded away.

I knew what he meant. Oddly enough I'd often felt drawn towards Chamonix ever since I'd spoken to Blake during our reading. In a way, he'd introduced me to the Alps. I wasn't going to forget that case in a hurry...

Five

It was the snow I remembered first. We have snow in Wales but nothing like this. Great blankets of white everywhere and little wooden chalets with icicles sparkling from the eaves, crowds of people in jewel-bright ski suits, swishing animatedly up and down the streets like flocks of tropical birds, and towering above the whole Christmas-card scene, the huge bulk of Mont Blanc. Chamonix took my breath away.

The trip had come about very suddenly, as these things often did. I was sitting in my office one morning, a bit bleary and trying to get my thoughts together before starting work when the phone rang and I heard Mum, who was sitting at the desk, say, 'That's okay, I'll get Diane. You'll be able to talk to her yourself.'

The next thing the phone was shoved into my hand and I was talking to a lovely lady called Sally.

'Diane! Could I have a reading with you?' she asked. 'I need to speak to you about my son Blake. He's gone missing.'

She began to say more but I stopped her quickly. 'Let's leave it there for now Sally,' I said gently, 'and we'll do a proper reading. I've got a client arriving in a minute and I don't want to have to cut things short so let's make an appointment for a full reading. In the meantime can you send me a picture of Blake?'

Shortly afterwards, a picture of a good-looking young man in Army uniform arrived, and a few days later I had a phone-reading with Sally. It was difficult because I had a strong feeling Blake was in the spirit world, which of course is not what Sally wanted to hear.

I had a fleeting impression of a handsome lad with strawberry blonde hair and a devastating smile.

'They said I absconded Diane!' he said indignantly. 'I didn't abscond. I'd never do that.' And I saw snow all around him. He was wearing his Army uniform.

'He was with his regiment when he disappeared,' I said to Sally, 'and he was somewhere very cold.'

'That's right,' she said.

'I do feel he's in the spirit world,' I added as kindly as I could, because of course, like any mother, I'm sure she was hoping against hope he'd just gone away somewhere and would one day walk back through the front door right as rain.

Even as I spoke, Blake was fading away and I couldn't hang onto him. 'I didn't abscond...' he insisted again as he went. This was clearly a very important point to him, but then he was gone.

'I think it might help,' I said slowly, 'if I went to the place where he disappeared.'

'That's easy,' said Sally. 'It was Chamonix in the French Alps. I've been out there a few times since he disappeared. It would be wonderful if you had the time to come out with me.'

Which is how, a couple of weeks later, Mum and I, wrapped up very warmly, found ourselves on a plane heading to Geneva. Sally and her husband met us at the airport, and we shared a car to the Alpine town of Chamonix. It was a long drive, and snowing very heavily, but the roads were good and we chatted away the whole journey, though we took care not to talk about Blake. Sally and her husband were a delightful couple, and so kind to Mum.

Eventually we arrived at the hotel Sally had booked. It was a beautiful old building with big shutters on the windows, and Mum and I were shown to a cosy room with a little balcony overlooking the street. Mum and I gratefully dumped our suitcases. We were pretty tired by now and it was already dark outside, but Sally was keen for us to visit the place where Blake was last seen.

'Are you alright Diane?' asked Mum. 'You shouldn't be doing this now. You're tired.'

This was true but I could understand that parents with a missing child just need to know what happened.

'It's fine,' I told Mum. 'I'm okay. Let's go.'

It was bitterly cold outside, by now, and I was afraid Mum would slip on the ice, so I hooked her arm through mine and the four of us set off up the road. Suddenly Blake appeared in front of us, though the others couldn't see him.

'It was this way,' he said, nodding to me, and he began threading his way through the crowds, gesturing to me to follow. I hurried to keep up with him, and Sally and her husband fell in behind. We walked on up the street until eventually we came to a club, all brightly lit up now, and busy with laughing tourists, eager for a little après-ski. Blake stopped and indicated the way he'd gone in.

'We loved Chamonix,' he said. 'We went in there, me and some mates. We were drinking heavily most of the night, having a good time.'

He was based near the town, on some sort of Army mountain training exercise, it seemed. I got a sudden picture of Blake a few hours later. He was with some other men – possibly people he'd met in the club – but now they were tottering out, clearly drunk. It all seemed to be good-humoured. They were larking about all over the pavement, playing pranks on each other and generally enjoying themselves in that boisterous way fit young men do when they've had a few drinks, as they headed off up the road.

'I just wanted to get back to my tent and get some sleep,' said Blake. But somehow, as the group headed out of town the happy mood evaporated and the horseplay turned nasty. 'Then there was an argument,' Blake went on. 'There was a bit of pushing and shoving and I was knocked backwards. I ended up falling and banged my head on a big rock. And watch this…'

Suddenly the street around me disappeared and I was looking at a dark place in the countryside. The sound of water rushing by was loud in my ears, then two men carrying a body between them, stumbled out of the night. I watched as they hauled their heavy load across the uneven grass towards the river. Then, staggering a little as they tried to keep their balance on the slippery bank, they swung the body, heaved it up and tossed it out into the freezing black water. There was a splash and then it was gone.

'They had to get rid of the body Diane,' said Blake. 'My body! Please tell Mum and Dad I love them, and that they were right. I didn't run away. I would never, ever run away. They were right.'

The ugly scene vanished and I was back on the pavement outside the nightclub. I felt sick and a bit dizzy.

'That's all I can do for now Sally,' I apologised. 'I think I need something to eat.'

'Oh of course!' said Sally. 'You must be starving. Come on. We know just the place.'

We ended up in a snug, Alpine restaurant where Mum was fascinated to try fondue for the first time. There was a lot of laughter over the table as we all tried to wind the warm cheese round our spears of bread and vegetables, but naturally Sally wanted to talk about Blake as well.

'So you think he's been murdered, Diane?' she asked.

'Not exactly,' I said. 'I don't think they set out to kill him. It seemed like there was an argument that got a bit physical. He was pushed and fell and cracked his head badly on a rock. I think it was an accident. But two of them decided they must get rid of his body. They're the ones that threw him in but I feel all of them knew exactly what happened that night.

They've just made a pact not to say anything.'

'The trouble is, everyone seemed to have been drinking quite a bit,' said Sally's husband, 'so it's very difficult to find anyone now with a clear memory of what happened that night.'

At least the couple seemed to have accepted that Blake was dead and not hiding away somewhere, so my account of his words wasn't a complete shock. 'The Army told us he must have run away,' said Sally, 'because it would be impossible for someone to disappear so completely, without a trace, unless it was deliberate. But we knew Blake would never abscond. Now we just want to find his body and take him home.'

'We've got another psychic working on it too,' added Sally's husband.

'Well don't tell me anything they said!' I said. 'I don't want to be influenced in any way.'

They were very keen on trying to find the place I'd described, where I'd seen the two men throw Blake's body into the water, so the next day we drove up and down this big river.

Some distance outside Chamonix, at a town called Bonneville, I felt drawn very strongly to an area beside the water. We climbed out of the car and trooped to the snowy bank. I don't know what we expected to see after all this time, but of course there was nothing but the wide, khaki river swirling by. I stared at the powerful current sweeping along and felt suddenly helpless. There was no way we were going to find Blake's body like this.

The only thing we could see was a little weather-beaten old man in a flat cap, busy at the water's edge with some kind of machinery that appeared to be sieving the flotsam and jetsam washed along by the flow.

To my surprise Sally seemed to know him. 'Yes, I've met him a few times when we've been over,' she said. 'He was so upset to hear about Blake, he wanted to help. He's been keeping an eye on whatever the river brings along for us.'

The old man didn't speak any English and Sally and her husband only a little French but they greeted each other warmly and he showed them the debris he'd been sifting through that day. Nothing that had any relevance to Blake of course.

I felt deflated. There was nothing more I could do here it seemed. I couldn't see anything else, beyond Blake being thrown into the water.

'Don't worry. It won't be long Diane,' said Blake suddenly into my ear. 'They will have evidence very soon. There will be proof that I was put into that river. I don't think the other men will ever say what happened the night I was killed though. They won't admit it. It's funny: I always thought I'd like to live here. Now I'm stuck here - dead!'

We were sitting in a nearby café by this time, warming up after the mountain cold. All of us a little dispirited, I felt.

'Blake very much wants closure,' I assured Sally, 'And he seems to think you *will* get evidence despite what you've been told. In fact it's going to come to light very soon. *Very* soon.'

Sally smiled wistfully. We all wanted it to be true, but to be honest, none of us could imagine what could possibly change.

There was nothing more to be done. Mum and I headed back to Wales. Soon other cases claimed my attention and Blake and Chamonix began to fade from my mind.

Then one day, a few weeks later, the phone rang. It was Sally.

'Diane, d'you remember the old man who was sieving the water on the bank at Bonneville?' she asked.

'Yes of course I do,' I said. 'The kind man who couldn't speak English.'

'That's right,' said Sally. 'His name's Joseph. Well guess what? He found a bone. A human bone. We think it could be Blake's. What d'you think?'

'Yes!' I said instantly. 'You're right. It's his. This is the evidence he was talking about. He said it would come to light very soon.'

The family had to wait for the scientific tests to be carried out of course, but not long afterwards it was confirmed that the bone found was a human femur – a thigh bone – and it belonged to Blake.

It was closure, of sorts. Not the sort, sadly, that Sally really wanted because it's unlikely we'll ever know from the other people involved exactly what happened that night. But at least it was confirmed that Blake hadn't absconded and that his body ended up in the river – just as he'd told me.

So sad too that Blake never got the chance to fulfil his dream of living in Chamonix amongst the mountains he loved so much. I sighed. I could certainly understand why he admired the place. It was beautiful. I wouldn't have minded living there myself, but right now I had to be practical.

And the funny thing was, even though, ever since our troubles began, I'd been regretting the fact we hadn't managed to sell the farmhouse and so ended up with two mortgages to pay – now I realised the farmhouse was a blessing. Grandfather had been busily keeping buyers away because he knew I'd need it! So, just as my dream house went on the market, our farmhouse tenant decided to leave, which meant that very soon Liam and I could move back into the place, ourselves. We wouldn't be homeless after all.

It took a while for the big house to be sold, but once I'd moved our furniture back into the farmhouse it immediately felt like home. Almost as if we'd never left. If it wasn't for the fact Peter was thousands of miles away, I could have half believed it was the early days of our marriage again, instead of me being alone, uncertain and wondering whether the only answer was divorce.

As usual I tried not to think about it and concentrated on working hard to pay the bills. I was very busy with my readings, but after work most weeks, I also went round to Beryl's to give her healing.

It was odd the way I'd met Beryl. Not long after Mixed Blessings was published, I was doing a book signing at a pretty little bookshop in the ancient Welsh town of Carmarthen, legendary birthplace of the wizard Merlin, and conveniently not far from where I was living.

As I sat there, scribbling away I noticed an older couple join the queue. The woman was particularly striking. Smartly dressed, with matching jumper and cardigan, she had silvery white hair and the biggest, bluest eyes I've ever seen.

When she finally got to my table, she put down her book and opened it for me to sign but I could see it wasn't really an autograph she was after.

'Diane, I need your help,' she said, fixing me with that beautiful sky-blue stare.

'It's healing you want isn't it?' I asked, though I already knew the answer.

She nodded. 'I've already read your book and I know you do healing,' she said. 'Can you help me?'

I knew instantly she had cancer but I asked her anyway. 'You've got cancer, is that it?' I asked gently.

She nodded sadly. 'Breast cancer.'

'Well of course I'll gladly try to help,' I promised.

I'd never actually set out to be a healer. I'd discovered the gift quite by chance. One day I was doing a reading when I suddenly realised the lady sitting in front of me was in great pain from a bad back.

'Do you have back problems by any chance?' I asked.

'Yes I do,' she said. 'My back's killing me!'

As she spoke, I could feel my hands start to tingle and warmth run down my fingers. The next second, I knew I absolutely must take this heat and put it on the lady's back. I stood up and went round behind her. I didn't actually lay my hands on her back, just put them very, very close. Instantly the heat flamed up. It felt like my palms were on fire. I held them steady, close to her back, willing the warmth to radiate through her clothes and into the trouble spot.

'Hey!' said the lady after a minute or two. 'My back's getting very warm!'

I didn't know how long it would take but after a while the glow began to subside so I reckoned the moment was over. I returned to my seat, my palms cooled and the woman declared her back felt much easier.

A few months later she wrote to let me know she'd enjoyed her reading but better still, she'd had no trouble with her back ever since. I was so thrilled, I tried the same exercise with Mum, who also suffered with her back from her days working in a restaurant, heaving heavy saucepans around and being on her feet all day. She'd been in such pain the doctor sent her for an X-Ray and it was discovered the discs in her spine were hopelessly worn. Instead of the plump little round cushions they were supposed to be, Mum said the X ray showed the discs now resembled thin slivers of half-moons.

There was nothing to be done, Mum was told. She had to resign herself to living on Co-codamol forever. Yet after a few sessions of healing, Mum too was able to throw away her pain-killers and even take up dancing again.

It was wonderful to be able to help like this, and little by little I found myself doing regular healing sessions – for which I never charged - as well as readings.

So of course I was happy to work with Beryl, though deep down I knew she couldn't be cured. She'd been told she had around six months to live. The most we could hope for with the healing I knew, was to extend that cruel deadline.

Beryl and I soon became great friends. I'd go over to the

couple's comfortable bungalow in Carmarthen almost every other day, and after the healing, Beryl and I would chat for ages. She really was just like the grandma I never had.

It's funny, I'd always longed for a grandma. A proper, cuddly grandma with silver hair, a kindly smile and a patient, listening ear. The kind of grandma who bakes tasty cakes, worries you're not eating enough and is always on your side. The sort of grandma you read about in books.

Us kids all longed for a grandma in our family because we'd never had one. Mum's mother had died in a freak accident before we were born and my father's parents had split up years ago and his mother moved to Scotland. We'd never met her.

I'd ended up semi-adopting someone else's grandma – a sweet old lady who lived round the corner from our home in Swansea. I loved to pop round to her little house after school and sit chatting in her kitchen, telling her all about my day and what we'd been up to in class. I helped with any chores she needed doing and trimmed her hair for her when it was getting in her way. I adored playing hairdresser! But of course, I knew she wasn't really my grandma. She was only borrowed.

Then one day, momentous news arrived. Grandma was coming to visit! Our real grandma, all the way from Scotland.

We were so excited. Mum cleaned the house from top to bottom and polished the spare bedroom till the whole house reeked of lavender. The guest bed was resplendent with our best sheets, crisply ironed, the pillows plumped. Debbie and I went out to pick a big bunch of wild flowers for grandma to enjoy on her dressing table.

Then, on the appointed day, the car stopped outside our house and we all raced to the window to see Grandma arrive. The car door swung slowly open and as we watched, hardly daring to breathe, out stepped – not a grey-haired little old lady but a tall, rangy figure with garish dyed-blonde curls, high heels, bright nail polish and a cigarette clamped in its ring-encrusted fingers.

Our mouths fell open in horror. Who was this woman and what had she done with Grandma?

'This *is* your grandma,' Mum hissed at us. 'Behave yourselves.'

The fake grandma continued to disappoint. She swept into the house and stared around with disdain. Upstairs she didn't even appear to notice the flowers we'd picked, or the beautifully ironed sheets. She slung her suitcase on the bed, kicked off her shoes and said she thought she'd like a rest now. 'It's been a helluva journey.'

As for her delightful, unknown grandchildren – she didn't seem interested in us at all. We all trooped out.

As the days went on Grandma showed no inclination for baking jam tarts with Debbie and me, or watching the boys ride their bikes, or admiring any of our drawings. As for reading us a story – forget it. She spent a lot of time in her room or out shopping with Mum. I'm not sure she even mastered our names. Well, there were *four* of us!

We were all relieved when it was time for her to go back to Scotland. After she'd gone, Debbie and I went into her bedroom. The flowers we'd picked had been shoved out sight behind the curtain on the window-sill and in their place stood an overflowing ashtray. Under the bed were several empty vodka bottles.

Debbie and I looked at each other.

'That wasn't a real grandma!' said Debbie.

'No,' I said, 'I think she was a witch.'

So now after all these years, how lovely to have a proper grandma-figure in my life. Just heartbreaking that I knew I wouldn't be able to enjoy her for long.

Beryl was so appreciative of the healing and it was a joy to see her gradually improving day by day. It bothered her though that I wouldn't take any money for the work.

One afternoon I happened to mention how nice she looked in a brand new lemon jumper. The colour really emphasised the blue of her eyes and the sleek silvery-white of her hair. Next time I arrived, she had a parcel for me – an identical jumper, in a different colour.

'It's beautiful Beryl!' I said, stroking the soft, pretty wool. 'But you shouldn't be spending your money on me.'

'Yes I should!' she insisted. 'You won't take a penny otherwise and I'm so grateful.'

At Christmas she gave me a present which seemed to be a picture, but when I opened it up, I found a framed acrostic poem of my name that she'd had specially made. The sweet sentiments she'd attributed to each letter of Diane brought tears to my eyes. Of course it went on the wall straight away.

We were all so thrilled when it was found Beryl was in remission. Beryl was overjoyed. She thought she'd beaten the cancer once and for all. I knew she hadn't but I kept my thoughts to myself. I didn't want to spoil her happiness. The important thing was to enjoy every day, and Beryl did.

One afternoon I arrived to find her bubbling with excitement. She'd been invited to take part in a semi-nude photo-session for a cancer survivor's calendar to raise money for charity– rather like in the film, Calendar Girls.

'Who'd have thought I'd be asked to be a pin-up one day!' laughed Beryl. 'What d'you think Diane? Should I do it?'

'Of course you should do it!' I said. 'You'll be fabulous!'

A few weeks later I received my complimentary copy of the calendar and there was Beryl - a beaming Ms March, eyes sparkling with fun, and a large bunch of daffodils strategically placed across her boobs.

In the end Beryl survived for three years – a big improvement on the original six months. The last few weeks were immensely sad, as these things always are. I carried on giving her healing to ease the pain right to the end, and she never lost her forthright sense of humour, despite everything.

I was devastated when she finally slipped away, though I wouldn't have wanted her to suffer any longer. I couldn't face going to the funeral. I'd been to too many and I knew Beryl would understand. In fact, not long afterwards, she told me herself.

I'd been dashing over to Carmarthen for our healing sessions for so long it seemed strange when suddenly I could just go straight home instead. One evening I found myself sitting there, at a bit of a loose end, thinking about Beryl and the things I'd like to tell her, when suddenly I heard her voice. I looked round and there she was, for a fleeting moment, outlined in the doorway.

'Cheer up love,' she said, smiling at me, the same old smile. 'There was no need for you to be at the funeral. I'm fine and it's going to turn out alright. You'll be okay.' And with that she was gone.

Six

Work was carrying on in the same old way, despite the ups and downs of my private life. Whatever I felt about the difficulties with Peter and the grief around Beryl, I still had to get on with it. There were people out there who needed my help.

One of the results of taking part in the Britain's Psychic Challenge, and the various magazine articles that followed, was that I received hundreds of letters and emails from all over the world. Far more than I could cope with on my own, which is where Mum's help was invaluable. She came with me to the little office and spent the day cheerfully opening letters and answering the phone.

One morning, Mum was working her way through the pile of mail, as usual, while I made us both a drink. When I looked up, I noticed she'd stopped ripping envelopes and was over by the window, examining what looked like a photograph.

'What d'you make of this Diane?' she asked, turning round and holding it out. 'There's definitely something there.'

I wandered across and stared over her shoulder. The snap showed a teenage boy striking a jokey pose in a typical teenager's bedroom, but to the side of him you could just make out the fuzzy shape of what appeared to be an elderly man in old-fashioned clothes. He seemed to be watching the boy in the picture, and presumably, looking past him, at the person behind the camera.

Oddly enough the old fella even looked a bit like my great great grandfather, I thought. But then I expect we'd think most elderly gentlemen from those days would look similar to us now.

I picked up the letter that accompanied the photo. It was from a boy in Scotland named John. He'd taken the picture of his friend that day, he said, and when they looked at the photo afterwards they were amazed to see what seemed to be an old man standing behind him – despite the fact there was no one else in the room with them at the time and they hadn't been aware of him at all.

John had read about me in a magazine, he explained, so he thought I'd understand, and be just the person to tell them what was going on. Did I think they'd captured a ghost on film? And if so, did it mean the family house was haunted?

I looked at the photo again. Benevolent vibes wafted out from the dim figure. There was no harm here intended for young John. This was more like a grandfather watching over a much loved grandson.

'Could you tell him, Mum there's no need to worry,' I said handing the letter back to her. 'That *is* a spirit in the picture but it's a grandfather figure in his life, coming close. It's a good sign for him. I feel too that John has a lot of psychic ability himself and that's why he was able to capture the man with his camera.'

So Mum let John know the good news and I assumed that was the end of it. But a few days later we heard from John again and though he couldn't have known it – his polite thank-you note turned out to be a complete bombshell.

'Thanks Diane,' he said innocently. 'That's good to hear. I'm doing some research into my father's great grandfather – a Ronald Owen Preston, who worked on the railways in Africa – so maybe it's him.'

I nearly fell through the floor when Mum told me. How incredible was that! A boy in Scotland somehow photographs a ghost, and decides, out of all the psychics in the UK, to send it to one who's a complete stranger, hundreds of miles away in Wales – who turns out to be a long lost relative! Who turns out in fact, to share the same great great grandfather.

I rummaged through our files and found our copy of John's photograph again. I peered closely at the misty figure of the old man in the background. No wonder my first thought was he looked very much like my great great grandfather. He *was* my great great grandfather!

It could have been an amazing coincidence of course but I don't believe in coincidences. I thought back over the past few years to the day I discovered the identity of the Lined Man who used to appear to me as a child. Once I'd realised he was none other than Ronald Owen Preston, the renowned railway engineer, and my great, great grandfather, like John, I'd spent a lot of time trying to research his background, but it was hard going.

Naturally there were quite a few historical references to the building of the famous railway and I even found a few letters written by Ronald himself, which had been preserved in various museums. In them, he described how he'd been orphaned as a young boy in Liverpool, and ended up being sent to a boarding school-cum-orphanage in India. When he grew up, he trained as an engineer on the Indian railways, and he also fell in love with Florence, his headmaster's daughter. Later, he was chosen to travel to Africa to work on the crazy new railway line and he took his new wife, Florence with him.

I knew too that my own father was descended from Ronald and Florence's grandson, and I'd found out that in later life, Ronald remained in Africa, remarried and had a second family. When he finally passed away in the 1950's at the age of 86, Ronald, 'the Railway Pioneer,' was even featured in the Nairobi newspapers. The puzzling thing was, I could find no further reference to Florence.

Beyond one evocative photograph of the intrepid young woman ceremoniously hammering in the last rail, as the line finally reached its termination at Lake Victoria, poor Florence seemed to have vanished from history.

We could find no record of her death, nor where she was

buried. Try as I might, I seemed to have reached a brick wall. By the time John got in touch, I'd long given up. I just accepted that the whereabouts of Florence, my great, great grandmother would have to remain a mystery.

And then along came John with his strange photograph! If I thought the spirit world couldn't surprise me anymore, I was wrong! It seemed Grandfather was determined that, one way or another, the story should come out.

The next thing I knew, John's aunt, having heard about the episode with the photo from her nephew, got in touch. 'Hello Diane,' she wrote, 'I think we're related!'

She turned out to be a lovely lady, named Fiona, who worked as a librarian in Scotland. And she was quite right. We *were* related, it was just that Fiona came from a different branch of the family. I think that makes us distant cousins of some sort.

'Ronald and Florence had three children,' Fiona went on. 'My grandmother was the youngest of the three, a little girl born much later than the two boys. She was called Florence after her mum. They christened her – Florence Emma (after Ronald's mum) Pearl.'

Fiona explained that though her grandma, Florence junior, was born in Africa, Florence senior took her back to India when the little girl was only two. Florence and her daughter – known to the family by this time by her middle name of Pearl, possibly to avoid confusion – then stayed on in India, with Florence's wealthy family. Eventually Pearl grew up, married a Scottish soldier stationed nearby and when he returned to Scotland, Pearl went with him. Florence senior remained in India for the rest of her life.

'So that explains why we couldn't find any mention of her grave in Kenya!' I said. 'It always bothered me that she didn't seem to have been buried by my great great grandfather.'

'Over here in Scotland, we just knew my grandmother as Pearl,' said Fiona, 'and apparently when she first arrived, the neighbours called her the Indian Princess because she'd been brought up with servants and didn't even know how to brush her own hair. Oddly enough, she looked very much like you Diane!'

It was astonishing. Fiona sent me some wonderful sepia photographs of Pearl's Indian wedding in the early 1930's, and there, amongst the smartly dressed guests and potted palms, was my great great grandmother, Florence. Stouter now, and much older of course, but still unmistakably Florence.

The puzzling thing was there was no sign of Ronald. He clearly hadn't attended the wedding and Pearl didn't seem to have spoken about him.

So what went wrong? How could that apparently devoted young couple have ended up living on different continents? After following him halfway across Africa, living in a tent for years and enduring who knows what hardships along the way, what had made Florence leave her husband and return to India?

It was a real puzzle, and one day, pottering around my lounge I came across the picture I'd seen in Kenya of Ronald and Florence sitting under the awning of their tent in the African bush. I'd taken a quick snap of it with my phone, so now I had my own copy. I picked it up and gazed at it closely. There they were, very much together, looking perfectly content in each other's company. What Florence made of Ronald's hunting trophies spread all around them I couldn't imagine but I suspected she liked the zebra-skin rug.

Funnily enough *I'd* got a faux zebra-skin rug too. It's not real but it's certainly a very good imitation. I've always been attracted to zebra stripes. As a small girl, my Auntie Trixie once came up to me, with her hands behind her back and a big smile on her face.

'Choose a hand! Left or right?' she said.

Instantly the image of a zebra flashed into my mind. 'Left!' I said, giggling at this fun game.

Auntie Trixie slowly drew out her left arm and there, dangling from her fingers was a small, neat handbag, covered in curvy black and white stripes, just like a zebra. My very first handbag. I loved it on sight, and that bag and I became inseparable for months.

I smiled at the memory. I'd often used black and white striped touches around the home ever since. In fact, I was thinking of revamping the kitchen in black and white right now.

'Oh yes, I'd love that,' said a voice behind me.

Startled, I turned and there, standing right behind me, was Florence – clear as day. It gave me quite a jolt. She looked just like she did in the picture I was holding. Upswept dark hair, crisp white blouse, slender waist and long, narrow skirt.

'Yes I belong to you,' she said, nodding. 'I'm Florence.'

The older, stouter Florence from Fiona's wedding photos had vanished away. This was Florence in her prime. Funnily enough I could even see a resemblance between us. I'd inherited her thick, dark hair and there was something about the shape of her eyes and nose that was very similar to mine.

I took these little details in in a flash, because more than anything, I was just so thrilled to see her. After all these years of being in contact with Grandfather, I'd never once been able to communicate with Florence, and now, suddenly, here she was.

'It takes me a while to get to know people,' said Florence, 'but it's time you saw me Diane and I want you to know I've always helped you.'

'I was just… looking at you,' I said, holding up the photograph I'd been gazing at. 'You and Grandfather. Outside the tent. You look so happy here. What happened between you? Why did you end up living apart?'

Florence sighed. 'I couldn't stay in Africa,' she said. 'I loved your great great grandfather very much. He was a wonderful man. But after a while, for me, Africa was not where I wanted to be. But Ronald loved it. He was busy with the shop he ran by this time, after leaving the railway. He was also doing readings in the back of the shop, in the evenings, and he was writing a book about his life. He had many friends from the construction days, who'd stayed on too. He was busy and happy.

'But my mother in India was ill and I was missing India and my family so much. I went home to be with my mother. Obviously, I took little Pearl with me. Mother had never even seen Pearl until then. Ronald junior was at school there too and I'd missed so much of his growing up. So I went back to India and ended up staying. It felt like home, while Africa did not. I didn't feel safe in Africa.

'I did love your Grandfather dearly but I knew he loved Africa. As soon as he arrived there, he fell under its spell. He never wanted to be anywhere else. He never wanted to leave. I just couldn't share his feelings. When we'd gone out there we'd thought it was temporary and we'd go back, once the line was complete. But of course it took so long and by the time it was finished, Ronald wanted to stay. But home for me was always India and once I'd gone back, I couldn't face leaving again.

'After a while, Pearl was so settled I wrote to Ronald and told him I wanted to stay. He said he understood and he'd travel back and forth to see us. He meant it, I'm sure, but he never did keep it up. I knew it was too much for him.

'We wrote to each other and tried to keep in touch. But the letters got fewer and fewer and it got to the point where we just didn't bother. In the end I realised it was impossible for us to be together. I wanted him to have a good life so I told him to move on and find himself a new woman.'

Well he did that, I thought to myself as Florence smiled and drifted away.

That night I was still so excited that another piece of the jigsaw had fallen into place, I couldn't sleep. Florence had always been such an enigma but now her story was becoming clear too. And amazingly, when I looked in the mirror I could see I really had inherited a lot from my great great grandmother. There was quite a striking resemblance.

Then it hit me. Here I was, puzzling and puzzling over why Florence and her husband had ended up living on different continents – while all the time my own husband and I were *also* living on different continents! Could it be history repeating itself?

If we're not careful, I thought, Peter and I will end up just like Ronald and Florence, no longer bothering to keep in touch.

That was sobering. Though I'd often mentioned divorce to Peter when we were arguing over the phone, I wasn't sure I meant it. I was so confused. I wasn't happy with the way things were, but I don't believe in breaking up marriages, if they can possibly be saved. You take vows for a reason, I've always felt, and you should try your best to keep them. Could I say, hand-on-heart I'd done absolutely everything I possibly could to keep our marriage alive?

I had a sinking feeling that perhaps I hadn't. Maybe I owed it to both of us to give the relationship one last try? Suddenly everything became clear. We couldn't go on like this, that was perfectly obvious, so there was only one thing to do. Since Peter wasn't going to return to me in Wales, I'd have to move out to him in Dubai – for good.

Seven

The villa stood, white and sparkling, a little back from the road in one of Dubai's smartest residential areas. Gardens, bright with Mediterranean plants, neatly clipped hedges and feathery palms, softened the harsh lines of the street. Inside, cool ceramic floors, pale furnishings and gleaming bathrooms calmed the eye after the glare of the desert sun.

I couldn't fault the home Peter had rented for us, or the lovely white Range Rover that was parked outside. We could even have a cleaner, he'd told me. I wouldn't need to lift a finger if I didn't fancy it. But despite the luxury, I couldn't help feeling uneasy.

I'd given up everything to be here. The farmhouse was back on rent, my furniture in transit somewhere between Wales and Dubai. I'd handed back my office, cancelled my readings and said goodbye to Mum, Debbie, my brothers and my friends. Liam was happily lodged with his best schoolmate during term time and all set to fly out to join us every holiday. The rest of the family promised to come out when they could. What's more, Lisa was now working in Dubai too so I'd have the chance to spend far more time with her, which would be wonderful.

Everything was sorted. It was perfectly possible for me to live full-time in Dubai, I persuaded myself. I'd officially emigrated.

'You'll soon have as many new clients as you can handle,' Peter assured me happily. 'You can work out here just as easily as you did in Swansea.'

This proved to be true. It wasn't long before one or two readings for Lisa's friends blossomed into dozens, as astonished new clients recommended me to *their* friends. What's more, working in another country proved to be very interesting. The people might appear different on the surface, but at the end of the day, whether you're a sheikh or a kitchen maid, if you've lost someone you love, the grief is just the same.

It was also a joy to be able to see Lisa regularly again, of course. Whenever we were both free, we treated ourselves to girlie shopping expeditions in Dubai's lavish malls, frequent lunches out and we even got our nails done together – all the things I'd missed for so long and which were such a delight to me.

Back at the villa, the cleaner and I had become great friends, and since I love cooking, she was only too pleased to let me teach her some Welsh recipes into the bargain.

And then of course I kept in regular touch with Liam and Mum through phone calls almost every night. So on the surface, everything was going well with my new sunshine life. Could hardly be better in fact.

And yet… Though I tried to pretend to myself Peter and I had settled back into our old relationship and things were the same between us, as they were before – it just wasn't true. I don't know where it went, or even when it happened, but somehow that old loving feeling that used to sweep over me every time I looked at him, had just evaporated. When our eyes met, that familiar spark of electricity between us completely failed to ignite. At least, it failed for me. And try as I might to summon it back, nothing happened.

When we were out together I found myself getting a little bit bored with his conversation, where previously, I'd be interested in every word. Little things he said, or did, or wore, began to grate on me, for no reason at all.

I tried to smile, and chat brightly so he wouldn't notice; I didn't want to hurt his feelings, but inside I just felt flat.

The lovely villa didn't feel like home and this relationship didn't feel like a marriage.

Admittedly I hadn't been happy living in limbo, miles apart, the way we'd been living the last few years, but now I wasn't happy living together in Dubai either. Every morning I'd wake up and wonder - how long can I do this? Will things change? Or is this it now? Will I have to pretend, forever?

And somewhere deep inside, I heard Grandfather answer, 'This can't go on Diane. This isn't right and you know it.'

Liam, who'd always been a perceptive boy, noticed it right away when he arrived for the Christmas holidays. He saw straight through my contented act.

'Mum, you can't stay,' he said. 'You're not happy and you and Peter aren't close any more.'

He could see we'd both changed. Peter had found his feet and developed in a different direction. He'd got new interests and new friends, which was only natural, but it meant he was no longer such a good fit for me. I expect I must have changed too. How could I not, after all the problems and disappointments I'd had to struggle with on my own, for so long? I expect I'd become more confident and independent than I was before, and no longer such a good fit for Peter either.

With every day that passed, it became more obvious to me the marriage was over. The trouble was, I felt like I'd burned my boats. After moving my whole life out to Dubai, it would be difficult to reverse the entire process. Even more difficult to admit I'd made a mistake. And above all, I didn't want to hurt Peter. While I can't believe he thought our relationship was wonderful, I don't think he'd realised how unhappy I was.

In the end, I knew it had to be done. After the holidays were over and Liam had gone back to Wales, I finally plucked up the courage to tell Peter I wanted to go home, and that divorce was the only answer. I'd tried as hard as I could to save the marriage, I'd gambled everything on this one last chance, but it just hadn't worked.

Unfortunately, Peter didn't feel the same way. He would have been happy enough to carry on for longer, but I knew there was no point, it would only be postponing the inevitable.

Sadly, I repacked my bags and headed back to Wales. Sitting alone on the plane I realised I'd never completely understood that old expression 'with a heavy heart' until then. I thought I did, but now the words took on a whole new meaning. My insides really did feel so heavy, like I was carrying around a lead weight under my ribs. It's a terrible thing to end a marriage. I felt like I'd failed. Every time I thought about what I'd done, misery swept over me. Yet for me, there was no alternative. Just like my great great grandparents, Ronald and Florence, circumstances had forced Peter and I to live thousands of miles apart, and gradually, we'd fallen out of love.

I had no idea what I was going to do now. The whole future I'd envisaged had crumbled away and I had no idea what would replace it. I'd have to start all over again and I didn't relish the prospect, though there was nothing else to be done.

Mum and Debbie were thrilled to see me back of course. Liam was delighted and my friends were pleased, though perplexed. What was not to like about a luxury new life in the sun, they wondered?

It wasn't even as if I was running away from a cruel husband. Peter was a good man. It was just that he was no longer the man for me.

In many ways, despite the problems, I'd been incredibly lucky. It took me a while to recognise it, but a reading that came along soon after I'd returned to Wales brought that truth home to me rather forcefully.

That morning I'd noticed I had a reading booked in the diary for a woman who'd been very insistent on coming along. That wasn't unusual, so I thought nothing of it until the door opened, the lady walked in and instantly, the most beautiful young woman materialised beside her. She had honey blonde hair, big, caring eyes and her perfect make-up made her look just like a model. In fact, she was so gorgeous she could have been a model.

'I'm Sandy,' said the stunning girl. 'But I didn't do it Diane. He made me! He made me! Tell Mum and Dad, please. We'd been to London that day... I didn't like it. I didn't feel safe there and when we got back... he was so angry...!'

'You're here about your daughter aren't you?' I said turning to my new client. 'She's here and she's talking about having been to London.'

The woman, who'd been just about to sit down, jumped up again, eyes widening in astonishment. 'Hang on a minute. Can I just fetch my husband in?' she asked. 'He's just outside. He needs to hear this.'

'Of course. Bring him in!' I said.

A few minutes later the woman returned, with her slightly reluctant husband in tow.

'I loved my dad,' said the lovely young woman, turning to him with a smile. 'Ask him if he remembers how I used to sit on the arm of the sofa, polishing his glasses for him?'

'Yes! She did!' said the man, eyes filling with tears. 'She always did that. It's true.'

'And now my brother won't go to bed – he's too upset. He sleeps in the chair,' Sandy went on. 'Tell him to go up to bed. It doesn't help, sitting up half the night. '

'That's right,' her mum confirmed when I passed on the comment. 'He was so upset.'

Sandy went on to tell me the harrowing story of her awful husband. 'I didn't even want to marry him,' she explained, because by then she'd realised how cruel he could be, but it was too late. By the time the wedding was arranged, she was too scared of him to back out.

'No one would have guessed what he was like,' she explained, 'From the outside you'd have thought we were the perfect couple with the perfect life. A lovely house, two cars on the drive and everyone in the street thought he was wonderful. He was so nice to the neighbours. Always said good morning, shook their hands, always offered to help. Nothing was too much trouble. He'd even cut their grass for them as a surprise when they went away. They thought I had the kindest, most caring husband imaginable.

'But behind closed doors it was different. He was like Jekyll and Hyde – he turned into a monster when we were alone. He would never shout out loud in case the neighbours heard. Instead, he'd come up very close to my ear and yell right into my ear-drum. He told me I was fat and ugly and useless, that no one liked me, no one loved me, no one wanted me. I was a waste of space.'

As she spoke I had a sudden picture of a tall, wiry man, with a vicious look in his eyes and a nasty curl to his lip. As I watched, he was snatching a phone out of Sandy's hand and hitting the button to disconnect a call.

'You don't go running to Mummy!' he snarled, his face turning an angry scarlet.

'He kept accusing me of having an affair. Said I was a whore,' Sandy went on. 'He was like two different people and I was walking on eggshells round him all the time, scared of setting him off. It got so I dreaded coming home from work. I stayed in the office as late as I dared, but then he wanted to know where I'd been. I wanted to leave him so many times, but I was too scared. I'd even phoned the police many times but nothing happened.'

Eventually, Sandy bumped into an old boyfriend from years before and they became close. It was this man who encouraged Sandy to leave her husband for a better life. So finally, that fateful night, she summoned up the courage to tell him she was leaving.

Unfortunately for Sandy, the plan backfired. 'He went crazy,' said Sandy, 'He said he'd tell everyone I was having an affair, I was a whore, they'd all see me for what I was. The world would be a better place without me. Then, it was almost like he'd been planning for me to commit suicide.

He grabbed a bottle of pills out of the cupboard and was shouting in my ear, 'Take them, take them, take them! You're worthless! No one cares about you. Take them!' He wouldn't stop. Shouting and shouting in my ear, shoving the pills into my hand, shoving my hand to my mouth. I didn't even know what they were...'

I knew exactly the kind of behaviour Sandy was talking about. Her husband had been a man just like my own father. As she spoke I had a sudden vivid flashback to when I was seven years old and woken in the night by my mother's sobbing. As she broke her heart, I heard my father's furious voice shouting over the top, 'Go on! Go on! Do it! I'll call the police and tell them you're suicidal. They'll lock you up and throw away the key.'

They'd been out for the evening and I could smell the alcohol on my father's breath from right down the hall, in the bedroom I shared with Debbie.

The next thing I knew, my mother was running by, my father crashing unsteadily after her. She dashed into my brother's bedroom, threw open the window and leapt out, but fortunately the flat roof of the kitchen extension was just below. She jumped off that too and landed safely on the grass.

I don't think Mum was actually, truly suicidal at that point. My father, in a drunken rage, was threatening to wake us children and give us a good thrashing, so mum took it into her head to distract him as best she could.

Nevertheless, I could well understand how a violent bully could drive their victim to swallow an overdose against their will.

'He more or less forced the pills into my mouth,' said Sandy. 'Bellowing in my ear all the time. He wouldn't back off. In the end it was easier just to let them slip down. But do tell Mum and Dad I didn't want to do it. I didn't do it. He made me.'

The story was very traumatic for any parent to hear but Sandy wanted her parents to know the truth. She hadn't left them on purpose. If it hadn't been for that terrible husband she would still be with them.

Then I had a sudden vision of the young woman now, glowing with health and surrounded by children. She looked genuinely happy.

'I never had a family of my own,' Sandy went on, 'but now I work with the children over here.' And she threw her arm out proudly to show me the little ones she regarded as her own babies now. 'Oh and thank Mum and Dad for the bench,' she added. 'I often come to see them when they sit there. It's lovely.'

'Oh! No one knows about the bench!' gasped Sandy's mum. 'We bought one in her memory.'

So the reading finished on a happier note. But thinking about it afterwards, it made me realise that when it came to troubled marriages, compared with my mum and poor Sandy, I had very little to complain about.

Eight

The strange thing was, after my first introduction to the tragic Sandy, I was to see her many more times. She returns to me frequently. She's become what I call one of my 'gatekeepers' – helpful souls who come back to assist with certain readings where the person I'm trying to contact is finding the connection difficult.

I have quite a few spirit friends; some people would call them guides or gatekeepers – however you like to think of them – who help me like Sandy does, it's not just my Grandfather who visits. Different spirits turn up to suit different cases.

When I was trying to establish what happened to poor Blake in Chamonix, I was conscious of Mark Green, the missing murder victim I talked about in my first book, hovering nearby, helping Blake tell his story. Like Blake, Mark was a healthy young man who'd lost his life after a night out so perhaps that's why they had an affinity with each other.

Sandy tends to come along when the case concerns another woman who's been mistreated by a man, or men. The woman doesn't even need to have passed over.

This was exactly the case when, one morning, I got an urgent call from an old friend. 'Diane, I'm at the hospital.' She said, 'Can you speak to my friend Trisha? She's in a real state. She's been brought into the hospital and she doesn't know what happened to her. Can she call you?'

'Of course she can,' I said. 'Give her my number.'

A few minutes later the phone rang and a distressed Trisha was on the line. 'I'm in hospital Diane,' she said. 'I'm covered in cuts and bruises – black and blue everywhere! I've got a black eye, a big bump on my head, cuts on my hands and I'm really sore inside, but I don't know what happened to me.'

'Oh dear, how awful for you,' I said. 'What's the last thing you remember?'

'Well I went out yesterday afternoon to meet a guy from a dating site. We went to a pub, but I was so careful. I made sure I only had a glass of Diet Coke. I'd decided not to drink as I was intending to drive home. Anyway I finished my Coke, and I vaguely remember walking to another pub with him... The next thing I know I was in an ambulance and I've ended up in hospital but I have no idea what happened! I really need to know. Can you help me?' She was starting to cry.

'It's ok Trisha,' I said. 'Can you send me a picture of yourself right away? And I'll see what I can do.'

'My daughter's here with me,' said Trisha. 'She'll do it for me.'

Within minutes a photograph arrived on my phone. I stared down at an attractive woman with dark, wavy hair and a shy smile. Poor Trisha did not deserve whatever had happened to her that day, that was certain.

Instantly I was aware of Sandy moving in beside me. This was just the sort of case that made Sandy very angry. 'It's on the wall...' she whispered.

I glanced round. Already an image was forming on my plain white wall. There was Trisha, sitting at a table in a pub, with a glass of Coke in front her. Opposite sat what looked like a real gentleman. He was dressed in a smart suit, his dark hair was slicked back stylishly and he seemed very polite and attentive.

Trisha was clearly attracted to him. She was chatting and giggling and they appeared to be getting on very well. After a while, the gentleman spotted someone he knew, across the bar. Another dark haired man. Excusing himself courteously, Trisha's date stood up and walked over to his friend and they chatted for a while. At one point they both glanced over at Trisha and she assumed her date was pointing out the woman he was with.

Instantly I felt a piercing pain in my stomach. Something was very wrong with this innocent looking scene. Trisha's assumption was wrong. Her date was not merely pointing out the woman he was with. The two men were making arrangements to meet up again later – with Trisha as the evening's entertainment.

Quickly I called Trisha back. 'Do you remember that guy you were with, getting up and talking to someone he knew?' I asked.

'Yes, I do Diane...' she said slowly. 'I'm getting little flashbacks coming through.'

I glanced at the wall again. Now Trisha and her well-dressed date were walking up the road towards another pub, but Trisha was stumbling and swaying and the man had to take her arm to stop her toppling into the road. To any passerby it would have looked as if Trisha was drunk, but I knew her drink had been spiked.

The scene fast-forwarded. Now we were inside a different pub. Trisha was sitting at a table with her date, plus three other men. They were shoving another glass of Diet Coke in her direction and she was laughing and giggling and almost sliding off her chair. From the disapproving glances she was attracting from other customers, it was clear they thought she was hammered.

The pub faded from view and now we were out of doors again. Darkness had fallen and Trisha was being half dragged, still giggling, into a dimly lit alley. The next thing, her figure almost disappeared from view as she was pushed towards the ground and the laughing men passed her about between them, ripping off her clothes and assaulting her.

I didn't want to see any more. I closed my eyes to make the vision go away, then I opened them again and tried to find a way to explain the situation to Trisha.

'I'm sorry have to tell you this, but you were raped,' I said as gently as I could. How on earth can you break that sort of news in a way that's not upsetting? It's impossible so I had to plough on. 'It wasn't just your date. There were four of them,' I added, 'in an alley near the pub.'

Trisha was sobbing again by now but at last things were becoming clear for her. 'That's where I was found, they told me,' she said. 'In an alley with half my clothes gone, all covered in cuts and bruises.'

'You can't let them get away with this,' I said. 'Now you know what happened, you must go to the police. Hopefully they'll be able to track down the man you'd arranged to meet and once they get him, maybe he'll tell them the names of the others. They need to be stopped.'

Trisha tearfully agreed that this had to be done. It would take a lot of courage on her part to go through it all again with the police, and maybe, one day, give evidence in court, but she bravely decided to go ahead.

As far as I know the case is still ongoing.

Thinking it over afterwards, this distressing episode made me realise how often my work involves quite a lot more than simply putting people in touch with their loved ones in spirit – valuable though that is. These days I'm often called upon to solve a mystery or give people guidance. Trouble is, sometimes people only want me to tell them what they want to hear and occasionally they even try to manipulate a reading for their own ends.

I remember one man who was so domineering I felt sorry for his wife. He barged into my office, all red-faced and bossy, and jabbed one meaty finger at my tape recorder. I usually record my readings on a CD so clients can take them home and listen to them later. Many people find they get so much information they can't take it all in at the time, so it's good to be able to replay the session later to pick up any bits they missed. However, it was clear that simply filling in the gaps wasn't what this client had in mind from his CD.

'Before you start recording,' he ordered, 'I don't want you to tell me anything bad. I don't want you to tell me my wife and I are going to split up. I *do* want you to tell me if my wife's having an affair but I don't want you to put it on the CD. Stop the recording. And I don't want you to tell me anything bad about my business either. Just tell me all the good things.'

He was so determined and insistent, my heart sank. How could I do my job properly under so many restrictions? Until I got started I didn't know what I was going to see – if it wasn't roses all the way, this could end up being a very short session!

Yet I soon realised this man *did* want a proper reading, it was just that he wanted to make sure only the positive aspects were captured on the CD. Any less happy news was to be for his ears alone. He quite obviously intended to play the CD to his wife afterwards, and wanted to arrange things so she only heard the edited version.

I wasn't happy about this arrangement but since he was already here, I decided to try to get the reading over with as quickly as possible. I'd hardly got started when he said in a quiet but threatening voice: 'Stop the recording.'

I stopped it. 'I feel my wife's having an affair,' he said. 'What can you see?'

'No, she's not,' I told him, because I truly didn't feel she was. I got the impression she worked in the media and there were a lot of attractive people around her, but so far, she was faithful to him.

I started the recording again. 'You've got two beautiful children,' I said, 'and you're going to be moving soon, to a lovely old house. Somewhere that's been completely renovated.'

The man nodded quite happily and we managed to get to the end of the session without stopping the recording too many times.

I was very, very relieved.

'Can I make another appointment?' he asked, as we finished, and he was gathering up his CD, ready to leave.

I shook my head. 'I'm sorry,' I said, 'but it's not a good idea to come too frequently. You're likely to be told the same things. You'll get the same reading again. You need to allow quite a bit of time to pass before a second reading's worthwhile – and also it leaves appointments free for other people to have their first reading. I tell most of my clients it's best to wait about 5 years before they come back.'

I wasn't saying that just to get rid of him – although I was tempted! It's what I tell all my clients, because it's true. Unless something unexpected radically changes a client's life in the few months after a reading, a second reading will end up more or less the same as the first – which is a waste of time for both of us.

The man didn't like it of course. For a moment he looked as if he might argue but fortunately, at that second, Mum appeared at the door ready to shepherd him out. He hesitated a fraction, then shrugged irritably and allowed Mum to guide him away.

Thank goodness, I thought as he disappeared into the corridor. I was heartily glad to see the back of him.

Although, as it turned out, I hadn't. This was a man who was obviously used to getting his own way and wouldn't take 'no' for an answer. A few months later I looked up from my desk expecting to see, new client, Mr William Barton, walk through the door, when instead, I found myself staring at the familiar red-faced and bossy features of the man I'd been so pleased to get rid of earlier in the year.

'You're not William Barton,' I said, a bit accusingly, to be honest. 'Have you come in his place or did you give a false name for the appointment?'

The man did at least look a little ashamed. 'Sorry about that,' he said. 'I made up a name. I know you said to wait, but I had to see you. I was desperate. There was no other way.'

He was telling the truth about being desperate, I could see that. Sweat was pouring down his face, there was a wild look in his eyes — rather like a horse about to bolt and he was so agitated it was difficult for him to sit still in the chair. I could feel his unstable energy catapulting between anxiety and aggression and back again and I began to feel quite nervous being alone with him.

'Don't tell me anything bad,' he snapped before I could say anything, 'but I want to know if my wife's having an affair. Tell me now, before you put the CD in.'

I sighed. That part was the same. His wife was not having an affair.

'No she's not having an affair,' I said as soothingly as I could. I had a horrible feeling this man was on the edge of suicide. I could see his marriage was in trouble even though his wife was faithful and there was no one else involved, but I didn't want to say anything that might make him crack and take drastic action. 'But recently there have been... difficulties... in the relationship,' I added tactfully. 'Can I suggest you go and have counselling? I think counselling could make a big difference.'

As I stared at the wall the pictures were getting worse and worse. There was no way I could tell him this. I could see the man had financial problems with his business, he was drinking too much, he was being paranoid with his wife and she'd had enough of him. I was just wondering what I could say that wouldn't send him over the edge when he barked another order.

'Turn off the recording!'

I pressed the button. 'I want to know if my wife's going to take me to court,' he said, 'but I'm going to ask you on the recording, and I want you to say she's not going to take me to court.'

Instantly, I saw a picture of the courtroom and his wife walking towards it. So she *was* intending to take him to court for some reason, I realised – just as he feared.

The man jabbed the button down again. 'So, is my wife going to take me to court?' he said loudly into the microphone.

I didn't dare ignore his instructions. 'I don't think so,' I said vaguely, 'but I strongly suggest you get counselling. You need counselling and I'm sure it will help with these difficulties. Please tell me you'll give it a try.'

Once again I somehow managed to bring the reading to a close, calm the man down and get him to leave the building peacefully. Afterwards I was completely exhausted. His troubled personality had drained me totally. I was also very worried. This was not going to end well, I was quite sure.

A little later we read on social media that the man had played the CD to his wife.

'See, Diane Lazarus says it's all going to work out and you're not going to take me to court,' he told her.

Fortunately, his wife paid no attention. We heard she did take him to court in the end, for his controlling, abusive behaviour and they are no longer together despite the lovely house and the beautiful children. I only hope he will one day take my advice and get the counselling he so badly needs.

It's a sad fact of life that amongst the people who genuinely need readings to help with bereavement, there are a few others who come along for their own deluded reasons, and some even have borderline mental health issues.

I remember one man wanted to know about his 'fiancée', the love of his life. Were they destined to be together forever? Were they going to get married soon? Was the marriage going to be happy? How many children would they have? And what gift could he buy her right now, that she would be thrilled to receive?

Though the man was smartly dressed and seemed completely respectable there was something about him that made me uneasy. Nevertheless, I cleared my mind as I always do and stared at the wall asking for pictures of him and his fiancée.

To my surprise the images that began to form showed just the man alone in what appeared to be his bedroom. He was sitting at a computer staring at the screen on which a beautiful model was apparently shooting a lingerie commercial. She was wandering about in a fancy bra and pants, striking provocative poses for the camera.

Then I noticed that the walls of the man's room were plastered with posters and photographs of the same gorgeous woman. There was even a framed photo of her beside his bed. He could have been engaged to a glamorous supermodel, but I was quite certain he wasn't. Then I noticed the pain deep in his eyes.

The woman was his fiancée in his own mind only. Chances are, they'd never even met and she was completely unaware of his existence. It was all a fantasy and at some level he knew it, though he was trying hard to hide that knowledge from himself.

'I'm so sorry,' I told the disappointed man, as gently as I could, 'but nothing's happening today. I've got a bit of a headache and I think that's blocking the reading. My mother will give you a refund.'

He shuffled sadly away, yet strangely, behind his disappointment, I could sense a feeling of relief. Perhaps deep down he'd been afraid I'd tell him the truth and force him to face a reality he wasn't ready to accept. I do hope he went on to find a real life girlfriend.

And then of course, at times I can misunderstand what my wall pictures are showing me. I'll never forget the time a very well-spoken, very cleanly scrubbed gentleman settled himself down in my client chair. There were no bad vibes coming from him at all. But when the wall pictures began to roll, I recoiled in horror.

I could see cans of Red Bull energy drinks, brilliantly-bright white lights shining down and blood, blood everywhere. Then the man himself came into view and he seemed to be cutting right into a human head!

Shocked, I stopped the reading. My harmless-looking client was obviously some sort of maniac.

'I'm sorry,' I said backing my chair away in fear, 'I'm not going any further. All I'm saying is I'm seeing blood. Blood everywhere… heads being cut into and cans of energy drinks. I can't do any more.'

For a second the man looked bemused, then he burst out laughing.

'Well you're right,' he said, 'I do see a lot of blood and I do drink a lot of energy drinks. I'm a brain surgeon so I do cut into heads. Plus, the operations tend to be long, so in between, I have energy drinks to keep me going.'

He laughed and laughed at the idea he could be mistaken for a serial killer and in the end I couldn't help laughing with him. My fear dissolved. I wasn't sharing the room with a maniac after all, and with that reassuring news I was able to carry on and do a perfectly normal reading.

Nine

Spring had come at last. The sun was actually shining, the first daffodils – our national flower here in Wales – were bobbing about, all golden and optimistic in the lane, and I was back in the farmhouse.

Against all the odds, I'd come full circle: Liam was doing well at school and thinking about university, Lisa was enjoying her life in Dubai and here I was a single woman once again, back where I started, trying to rebuild my British career and pick up the shattered pieces.

At least I had Rocky, my ever-cheerful little dog to keep me company. I was glad to be back too, to be honest. I'd missed my family and friends, and exciting and glamorous though Dubai always is – it just wasn't home.

Fortunately, my lovely friends rallied round and organised hilarious 'Girls' Nights' so I wouldn't get lonely. And my old mate Peter Hall was keen to organise more of our psychic filming expeditions.

Peter is an amazing man. He started out as a policeman and towards the end of his career in the force, did some filming for them. He became so interested in camera work that he ended up freelancing for HTV – our local TV station – and since he'd also developed an interest in psychic phenomena, he'd taken to accompanying me on some of my more unusual jobs and filming the proceedings so we had a record of whatever strange events might occur.

One day, I got a call that I reckoned would be just the kind of case to interest Peter. A woman who'd had a reading with me a few months before, phoned in a panic. She was a single mum and had recently moved into a new home with her small daughter. But her little girl kept waking up in the night, screaming that people were coming into her room – despite the fact, that when her mum went up to investigate there was no one there and nothing had been disturbed.

'It's getting to be a real problem Diane,' the woman said. 'She's scared to go to bed and these nightmares or whatever they are, are getting worse. Last night she was hysterical. Can you come round and see if there's anything here? D'you think the house is haunted?'

'I'll come over and have a look,' I promised. 'Would you mind if we filmed whatever happens?'

'Couldn't care less if it means she'll sleep through the night!' said the mum.

As I expected, Peter was intrigued. He loves nothing more than grabbing his camera and going ghost-hunting. I don't think he's ever captured a spirit on film yet, but you never know. One day he might stun the world!

A few evenings later, Peter and I arrived at a neat, cream-painted, semi-detached house, on the edge of a small village. Peter pulled his camera bag onto his shoulder and we walked up the front path towards the green door. But as I raised my hand to ring the bell, I got a sudden impression of a big, chunky, much larger door made of solid, stained wood, right in front of me. It was almost like a church door, I thought. But even as the idea was flashing through my mind, the old door vanished and I was staring at the much smaller, modern affair once more.

'I think there was a different door here once,' I whispered to Peter, 'a big old wooden one. In fact, I think there was a different building altogether here, years ago.'

At that moment the green, 21st century replacement was flung open and my old client was framed in the doorway. She was a very pretty lady in her late twenties, with long fair hair and a relieved smile.

'I'm so glad you could come,' she said leading us into a

modern sitting room.

'It happened again last night. She was in such a state.'

I was just about to ask to see the bedroom where the problems were occurring when a voice whispered in my ear, 'They were arguing again last night – in here. Big argument. That's what started it...'

Hmmn. This haunting could turn out to be more complicated than I thought. 'Was there some sort of argument here yesterday?' I asked out loud.

The mum looked surprised, then a little guilty. 'Well yes. Me and my boyfriend are having a few problems at the moment. We did have a bit of a row last night. But nothing much, and my daughter was in bed by then.'

I looked at her more closely. Despite her careful make-up there was a faint purplish mark near her eye. 'Did it get physical, this row?' I asked.

'No, no, not at all,' said the mum. 'Well, he did push past me at the end and I slipped and caught my face on the door. But that's all – and my daughter was in bed. She wasn't even in the room.'

Chances are the child wasn't asleep, I thought to myself and heard the raised voices. 'Right,' I said out loud. 'Could I see the bedroom and talk to your daughter?'

Glad to change the focus of conversation, the mum led me upstairs. We walked into a pretty pink bedroom with various dolls and toys strewn about the floor and an angelic looking four-year-old sitting on the bed surrounded by teddy bears. She stared up at me with huge dark eyes.

'Hello!' I said, 'Your mum tells me people keep coming into your room in the night and you want them to go away.'

'That's right,' she said, swinging her legs over the edge of the bed. She spoke very well and very sensibly for such a little one, I thought.

'Can you tell me a bit about them?' I asked, 'What do they look like?'

'They're children!' she said. 'They come through over there,' she pointed towards the door, 'and they keep trying to take my toys.'

'Well we can make them go away,' I explained, 'but what we have to do is call them in and ask them to go away. I will ask them to go away but I need you to ask them to go away as well. We need to ask them together. D'you think you can do that?'

She nodded.

'Okay. Let's call them in then,' I said. I started to concentrate, and I presume the little girl did too, because the next minute, a freezing fog seemed to descend on the room and when I turned towards the closed door, a troupe of school-girls was walking straight through it – without the need to push it open first. In they marched, right through the woodwork, hand in hand, in neat pairs, all dressed for the street, in identical navy-blue double-breasted gabardines and navy blue berets on their heads.

Once inside the room, though, the orderly crocodile broke up as the children spotted the toys on the floor. With whoops of delight they dropped their linked hands and dived towards the dolls.

Instantly the little girl on the bed went from unusually mature and sensible to hysterical: 'Leave me alone! Leave me alone!' she screamed, bouncing about and throwing herself into her pillow. 'They're taking my dolls! Leave me alone!'

'We've both got to ask them to leave,' I reminded her gently, as I tried to calm her down, but it was no use, she was too distressed.

Glancing up I saw another figure hurry through the closed door. It was a tall woman, with a halo of mousey hair framing her own beret, and a thin, not very substantial coat wrapped tightly around her. She looked chilled to the bone.

'Girls, girls!' she cried. 'This is no way to behave.' And they must have heard her because the next thing, they'd dropped the toys and they all disappeared. Suddenly the room was empty and the warmth began to creep back.

'It's alright,' I said to the sobbing child. 'They've gone now.'

Downstairs I had a quiet word with the mum. 'I want to find out more about these children,' I said. 'Hopefully they've gone, but I think when you have these arguments, though you know they're nothing to worry about, your daughter wakes up and the voices make her feel anxious. The energy she's putting out draws the spirits in.'

I'd often noticed that people who suffered some sort of trauma in their lives, particularly at an early age, frequently end up becoming quite psychic. We all have a latent gift but it's as if a strong emotion when we're very young, switches something on in our brains. In my own case, of course, I had a very troubled childhood. My father even tried to send me back before I was born, so perhaps it's not surprising I developed strong psychic powers from when I was just a small child.

We said our goodbyes to the little girl's mum and headed back through the green front door. As we stepped over the threshold, I had another fleeting glimpse of the heavy, old earlier version. It whispered away in a trice, like a smudge of cigarette smoke hanging, almost invisible, in the air. But it was tantalising me.

The case was tantalising Peter too. As we started to make for the car, he suddenly stopped.

'Tell you what Diane,' he said, 'there's something going on, up at that village hall we passed on the way here. Why don't we look in and see if anyone can tell us more about the girl's house? I'd like to solve this mystery.'

'Me too,' I agreed, 'I get the feeling those children were from

London, not round here, and the woman with them was their teacher. I wonder how they ended up in Wales?'

'Well maybe some of the older villagers will remember something,' said Peter. Ever the detective, he loves to verify the information I get through. You can't beat finding the true facts, Peter always believes, even though sometimes it takes a bit of time and effort.

So we left the car and strolled on up the road, towards the church hall we'd noticed. As luck would have it, there wasn't a council meeting or anything official happening inside. Through the door we could hear what sounded like big band music filtering out, and we walked in on a good, old-fashioned tea dance in full swing.

Straight away, my eyes zoomed across the cheerful room to an elderly lady who was carefully carrying a cup of tea back to a table in the corner. She was probably the oldest person there, I thought, so if anyone remembered what happened in the past, hopefully it would be her.

We went over and politely explained what we were doing.

'So would you know what that building down the hill might have been years ago?' Peter asked. 'Was there something else there before those houses were built?'

'Oh yes,' said the old lady, 'it used to be a girl's school. During the war some children from a London school were evacuated there with their teacher.'

Apparently, the old building, presumably with its big wooden door, was demolished years later and an estate of new houses went up in its place.

So the old school had vanished without trace, and almost out of memory. Yet could it be that some of those wartime girls were so happy there, they kept on coming back?

I'm not sure if we succeeded in persuading the spirit children to stay away from my client's daughter and her toys – as the process was interrupted. But I heard that shortly after my visit, the mum and her boyfriend parted and the little family moved away. So unless a new occupant of that bedroom gets a glimpse of the toy hungry school-girls and their long-suffering teacher, I guess we'll never know.

It's a strange thing with schools I've noticed. Maybe it's something to do with a build up over time of all that youthful energy and strong, unguarded emotions, but whatever the cause, former schools do seem to leave an indelible mark down the decades.

Several years later, I was doing a show in the lovely surroundings of the Manor Park Country Hotel just outside Swansea, when all of a sudden, during a quiet moment, the temperature plummeted, and the sound of children's voices and girlish giggles could be clearly heard.

The room went silent as everyone looked round to see who'd brought the children in. But there were no children to be seen. The sounds went on for several minutes more. Everyone heard them, not just me. They were even captured on our recording equipment. After a while, the giggling faded away, the room warmed up and we were able to carry on as usual.

Later we discovered that years ago, in the 1920's, the building had been taken over by St Joseph's Convent School – a Catholic boarding school I believe. Of course it's been a very long time since any classrooms or dormitories were located in that attractive Victorian mansion, but by the sound of it, no one's told the children!

Strangely, even while they're still here with us on the earth plane, children often seem to have a sixth sense about the spirit world. Not long after the St Joseph's episode, I came across a spirit girl, called Beth, in one of my readings and she was so enthusiastic about my work that she insisted she wanted to stay close. From now on, she informed me, she was going to help me with my readings from over there!

Our meeting happened quite by chance. One morning I got

an unexpected client cancellation and, shortly afterwards, a woman, who I discovered later was Beth's mum, phoned the office to see if there were any appointments free. I booked her into the vacant slot and soon she was sitting in front of me, glad to have got an appointment but not knowing what to expect. Poor woman was clearly desperately sad and also shaking with nerves.

Fortunately, my room is in no way spooky. It's bright, airy and calm and the scent of the fragrant candles is very soothing. It wasn't long before I could see she was beginning to relax.

Almost at once, a movement on my viewing wall caught my eye and when I turned my head there was a lively, young girl looking back at me. She grinned and pointed out her striking black hair – 'Dyed it myself!' she said proudly – and her Egyptian-Goddess style dark eyeliner, framing deep brown eyes. 'Never went out without it.' She also swirled her quirky dress round over her clumpy boots to show me the things she liked to wear.

'I'm Beth,' she said.

And Beth was clearly an original.

'I always told them I'd die young.' She went on, 'But they wouldn't believe me. I couldn't wait to get back over here and I told them all the time.'

'That's right. She did,' her mum confirmed.

It must have been so difficult for her family to understand, but from a very early age, it seemed Beth just wasn't happy in this world and was longing to leave it. Could it be she never really lost the memory of the Spirit World she'd lived in before she was born, and was itching to get back? Was it a type of homesickness?

It certainly seemed that way. For years, for no reason anyone could understand Beth was depressed and didn't want to be here. She kept telling her parents she was going to a better place. No matter how her family and her boyfriend tried to help, nothing could dissolve that underlying sadness and longing for another place, that lay deeply buried in Beth.

'I only stayed as long as I did for Mum and Dad and our little dog,' she said. 'If it wasn't for them I'd have gone long ago. But I do love them so. Please tell them not to feel guilty. I'm really happy now and I'm in a beautiful place. But I love them and will always love them.'

Beth had tried several times to take her own life, she confessed, and eventually she'd succeeded — which pleased her, even though she was sorry her family were so sad.

She passed on a number of personal details to her mum which proved she was still nearby, watching what they did, but at the end of the reading she had a message for me as well.

'I'm so glad I've met you Diane. I love your work and I'm going to stick around now and be your new door-keeper. I'll help the other spirits get through. But if I talk too much, just tell me to shut up!'

And Beth's been as good as her word. Quite often during a reading I sense Beth's unmistakable presence hovering close, particularly when I'm talking to young people who are finding communicating a little difficult. Beth helps them sort out their thoughts and pass them to me. I wouldn't want to be without her now.

Ten

I couldn't sleep. It was pitch dark outside and very late, but no matter how I rolled back and forth round the bed, I just couldn't get comfortable. Annoyingly, I was genuinely very tired, but every time I closed my eyes, my mind started to race again.

'Try the radio,' Grandfather's voice murmured somewhere in the night.

Good idea, I thought, even though it meant getting out of bed and padding around to find the radio and then clicking through dozens of stations to find something I liked, that was still broadcasting at this hour – all of which risked waking me up even more!

Still, a few minutes later I climbed back into bed, clutching the radio, and settled down to listen to the late night show from our local station.

Of course, just as I suspected, far from making me sleepy, I was soon engrossed in the show.

It was some sort of on-air agony advice programme. Listeners were ringing the presenter to explain their problems and he would take in the details for a bit, and then dispense his own pithy words of wisdom.

This man had obviously been chosen for his straight-talking, down to earth approach. My jaw dropped as I heard him tell one woman that her disappointing boyfriend was a waste of space and she should dump him immediately.

'Why are you even still with him?' demanded the presenter. Then he ticked another caller off for taking drugs.

It was certainly a pull-no-punches style, but the callers didn't seem to mind. They obviously appreciated the honest, no-frills opinions.

It wasn't my way of working, I couldn't help thinking, but the presenter clearly knew what he was doing and his audience was quite happy. What a lovely job he's got, I thought as I snuggled back under the duvet. How interesting to be a radio agony aunt. Only, if I was doing it, I reckoned, I'd ask the spirit world for answers, so the advice wouldn't come from me, it would come from the spirits close to the caller.

And putting together my own imaginary radio show in my mind, I eventually fell asleep.

Next morning, I was running late, and as I hastily threw together a lightning breakfast, I ruefully told Grandfather that the radio hadn't been such a good idea. I got even less sleep thanks to that show, not more, I teased.

But once again I'd misunderstood Grandfather's intentions. I only realised what he was up to a few months later when I picked up the local paper and spotted a small story about how the presenter of the popular, long-running agony show was now moving on to other opportunities.

'Which means they're looking for another agony aunt,' said Grandfather in my ear.

It struck me then. If I hadn't put the radio on to help me sleep that night, I would never have thought of doing a psychic radio show, but now I had an idea all planned out. I knew what I had to do.

Quickly I got in touch with the radio station and explained what I had in mind. Fortunately, they were intrigued, and I was invited onto the late night phone-in show, presented by the charming DJ Chris Blummer, for a trial run to demonstrate how it would work. To our delight, it went very well and I ended up doing a weekly slot with Chris for the next eight years!

Assisting Chris in the studio was his colleague Ross, who was a born-again Christian, and a bit dubious about my beliefs.

But even Ross said he'd never seen anything like it.

Chris and I would start chatting and then Chris would invite the listeners to phone in with any questions they'd like to ask me. Instantly, every single light on the phone lines would start flashing and the switchboard would be jammed.

One night, a male caller asked, 'What colour car d'you see me driving?'

I glanced away at the wall and immediately saw the image of a silver car flash past.

Then a woman's voice tutted in my ear: 'And if he carries on driving the way he's been driving this evening he'll have an accident. He's going way too fast.'

'You're in a silver car,' I told the caller, 'and if you carry on driving the way you've been driving tonight, you'll have an accident. You've got to slow down. You're going too fast.'

'Oh my God!' he laughed. 'How d'you know I'm driving a silver car? That's spooky!' and he hung up.

The calls carried on flooding in for the next two hours. Then suddenly the producer said to Chris, 'Hang on a minute; you've got to hear this!'

The next second, the man with the silver car was back on the line. 'I just wanted to tell that woman – Diane, I think her name was – I just wanted to tell her she was spot on! She said I'd have an accident in my car. Well, I just have, just a few minutes ago! You're spooky Diane, you really are.'

Chris roared with laughter and I couldn't help smiling.

'Wow!' I said. My gift takes me by surprise half the time, it really does.

Another evening, a man with a Welsh accent so broad it was difficult to catch every word, phoned in. 'Diane, my wife's been told she can't have children,' he said. 'It's upsetting as we'd love to have a family. Do you think there's any hope for us?'

That's sad, I thought, as I turned to the little bare patch on the wall I used to see my pictures. After a moment or two, a toddler with silky dark hair and wide brown eyes beamed back at me.

'Well I don't know what you've been told or why,' I said to the man, 'but I feel your wife will be pregnant very soon. I can see you having a beautiful little girl. She's gorgeous, with very dark hair and big brown eyes. Adorable she is.'

Naturally the man was delighted to think their wish would come true, but obviously he was doubtful too. Doctors had assured his wife it was impossible for her to conceive, so it was difficult to see how my prediction could be right.

Nevertheless, he thanked me and went off to tell his wife.

I thought no more about it, but a few months later, he phoned the radio station again. He wanted to tell me the thrilling news: amazingly, against all the odds, his wife was pregnant and they'd been told the baby was a girl.

'And she's bound to have dark hair and eyes,' he added, 'because we're Asian.'

I also ended up doing a one-off phone-in show for a radio station in Birmingham. Kerrang Radio. It stands out in my mind for one amusing call.

A rather bored sounding man came on the line. Well it *was* late at night. Maybe he couldn't sleep either.

'I don't believe in all this,' he said. 'You'll have to prove it to me. Tell me something about where I'm going in my life.'

I glanced at the wall and was immediately shown a map of France. Then I saw an articulated lorry beginning to drive right across the map.

'You're going to France,' I said, 'and I see you travelling in a truck.'

There was a strange, strangulated cry on the other end of the line. Then the man started to laugh. 'I don't believe this,' he said incredulously. 'I'm in my truck right now. I've just stopped in the services, but I'm on my way to France. I'm literally just heading for Dover.'

The Kerrang DJ sitting beside me almost dropped his mug of coffee. I laughed. 'Well you did ask where you were going with your life!' I told the caller, cheekily.

It was all going well. The radio shows were popular and my readings were picking up again. I was just so relieved my work was returning to normal and didn't seem to have suffered from my brief spell of emigration. Though the same couldn't be said of me – or at least my body. I was certainly more relaxed now I no longer had to worry about the situation with Peter, but despite my calmer feelings, I still seemed to get so tired.

I'd start work in my office at 10am and by 2 pm I was so exhausted I had to go home to rest. The readings always did demand a lot of energy, but now they seemed more draining than ever.

What's more, I began to crave laverbread. Despite having the word 'bread' in its name, laverbread contains no actual bread. It's a traditional Welsh dish, made of seaweed. The seaweed is repeatedly washed, then boiled or steamed until it's soft and resembles dark green cabbage. Then it's minced and often rolled in oatmeal, ready to be formed into little flat cakes or patties. In Wales it's traditional to eat laverbread fried for breakfast with bacon, or even more traditional, with cockles. Yum!

Perhaps it's an acquired taste, but apparently the legendary Welsh movie star, Richard Burton, used to call laverbread 'Welsh caviar' and he loved it. Now I loved it too.

Ever caring Mum found an excellent stall in Swansea Market selling wonderful laverbread, and she used to buy big bags of it for me every Friday when she went to get her fresh fruit and veg. Yet no matter how much she brought, I'd get through it in days. I just couldn't get enough.

The thing about laverbread is that as well as being tasty, it's highly nutritious and particularly rich in iodine. So one day as I was tearing voraciously into yet another steaming plateful, it suddenly occurred to me that perhaps my thyroid wasn't working properly.

I looked it up on line and found that your thyroid is responsible for releasing quite a few hormones into your body – hormones that affect your weight, your mood and your fertility amongst other things – so if your thyroid's under par for any reason, you're likely to experience a lot of unwanted side effects. Extreme tiredness for instance.

Hmmn, I thought as I read that, well that's me – and guess what? To keep your thyroid humming along nicely, you need a certain amount of iodine in your diet – and here was me craving iodine-packed foods!

A few days after reading that, I went along to the doctor. 'I'm getting so tired at work Doctor,' I said, 'I think I need my thyroid checked.'

Perhaps I'm being unfair, but it seems to me that doctors tend not to like it when you tell them what you think is wrong with you. I suppose you can see their point. After all, they're the ones who've been to medical school and mostly, their patients haven't, but still, it does get a bit depressing when you're quite convinced of what's causing your problem and they won't believe it. As usual, this particular doctor, who hadn't met me before, was doubtful of my diagnosis to put it mildly.

'I don't think it's likely to be your thyroid,' he said. 'You don't seem to have any other symptoms. What line of work are you in?'

Perhaps he thought I had a physically strenuous job, but this was going to be awkward.

'Well, I'm a psychic and medium,' I explained. 'I give people psychic readings.'

His eyebrows shot up and he peered at me as if I'd suddenly sprouted two heads, or confessed to running a satanic cult, or something equally awful. 'Well we'll do a blood test,' he said hastily, jumping up from his desk and walking me briskly towards the door. He clearly wanted to get me out of his surgery as quickly as possible, 'Come back in a couple of weeks.'

So, blood duly taken, I returned in a couple of weeks to find the results showed my thyroid levels were extremely low, just as I'd predicted. Who knows what caused the problem? Maybe my thyroid had been affected by the years of stress I'd been under. No one could say. But I was put on thyroxine tablets – the standard treatment for underactive thyroid conditions – immediately.

It wasn't an overnight cure, but within a few weeks I was glad to find my energy levels were beginning to climb and soon I was back to my old self.

Wonderful. I was just happy to be feeling better. And I was getting used to this difficulty with doctors. It wasn't the first time and it wasn't to be the last, I was quite sure.

As time went by I began to notice another facet of my gift was developing. When I concentrated on a medical problem it was as if I suddenly had X-ray vision. I could actually see inside the body to the source of the trouble. It was slightly unnerving, but as long as you're not squeamish, rather fascinating too.

So when my knee began to hurt, and the pain started radiating up back, to such an extent it was uncomfortable to take Rocky for a walk or climb the stairs, I knew there was something badly wrong.

One morning, I had a long hot bath to ease the pain, then stared at my dodgy knee, willing it to reveal its secrets. After a moment or two, it was as if my eyes were spearing right through the outer surface of my skin, into the bony kneecap beneath. The kneecap seemed to be off-centre from this angle, and pushing it askew from behind, was what looked like a large round bubble – a cyst. There also seemed to be a tear in the cartilage. 'No wonder you hurt,' I told my poor knee.

So off I went to the specialist and explained the problem.

Same old reaction. He didn't exactly say I was a hypochondriac but you could tell he was thinking it.

'Well now Ms Lazarus, it looks like a bit of mild arthritis to me,' he said, after a lot of painful pushing and pulling of my leg. 'I'll send you for an X-ray.'

'I think I need an MRI scan,' I said.

'Well first things first,' he said, 'We'll start with the X-ray and then see where we go from there.'

You're wrong, I thought to myself, but there was nothing I could do. I couldn't force the man to order an MRI scan.

Knee X-rayed, the results came through. To my surprise the consultant received me in his office with an 'I-told–you-so' air about him.

'As I suspected,' he said, 'the X-ray shows some mild arthritis.'

'The X-ray's wrong,' I replied.

He smiled politely. 'Well that's what it shows,' he said. 'I'm afraid you're going to have to learn to live with it. I'll give you a steroid injection. Then I suggest painkillers and a course of physiotherapy.'

I knew he was wrong but to be fair, the steroid injection helped for a while. Then, when the pain returned worse than ever, I was sent for physiotherapy.

The physiotherapist examined me too.

'The pain goes right up to my lower back,' I explained. 'Could that be due to a cyst pressing on the nerves?'

'No, I don't think the back pain is connected,' she said. 'It could be down to the way you're walking to compensate for the painful knee. It's arthritis. The physio will help.'

So I obediently did all the physio they asked of me. And my knee was as bad as ever. Worse, if anything. I asked to see the consultant again. I had to put up quite a fight to get an appointment but eventually they agreed to let me have an MRI scan.

And of course the MRI scan revealed a big cyst behind my knee that was displacing the kneecap. The cyst had actually attached itself to the sciatic nerve which was causing pain to travel up to my lower back. To make matters worse, the displacement of the kneecap had caused the cartilage below to tear.

The consultant was absolutely amazed when he saw the results of the scan. 'What I don't understand,' he said, 'is how you're managing to walk at all with a condition like this. You'll need an operation. Probably more than one.'

Later I went back to my GP to discuss the findings. 'Do you remember I told you I thought the X-ray was wrong and I could see a cyst and a tear in the knee?' I said – probably a bit smugly. I have to admit I was enjoying it.

He went white. 'Ah well... medicine is not an exact science. We have to try one thing at a time...' he blustered.

Sure, he had to follow the rules. I understood. After all, he probably didn't come across many patients like me. But if only they'd taken me seriously, it would have been so much simpler.

Eleven

There was no doubt about it, Rocky wasn't himself. My ever perky, bright-eyed little teacup chihuahua wasn't finishing his food. He just sat in the corner of the sofa with a sad, droopy look on his face. When I tried to tempt him to play, he padded around his toys in a listless, half-hearted way just to humour me, but you could see he wasn't in the mood.

A few weeks before, he'd had a bad tooth removed at the vet's and he should be fine by now. In fact, the vet insisted he *was* fine now, but I knew differently. I stared at his sad little face and suddenly got a mental picture, almost like an X-ray of his jaw and teeth. Deep in his gum I could see sharp little fragments of tooth still embedded. No wonder his mouth hurt. No wonder he didn't want to chew his dinner. Every bite must have been torture.

Back we went to the vet. But it was the story of my knee all over again.

'He's fine,' said the vet.

'I don't think he is,' I explained. 'I think he needs an operation. There are bits of tooth still in his gum.'

The vet sighed and stared at me as if I was an annoyingly over-anxious mother fussing over her baby. An over-anxious mother with an overly-vivid imagination, at that. Nevertheless, he checked Rocky once again, feeling all round his mouth and jaw.

'Really Ms Lazarus, he's fine,' he said, straightening up. 'There's nothing wrong with him.'

Rocky shot him a wounded glance from the examination table. I'll swear that dog understands every word!

'Maybe his gum's still a bit sore from the extraction,' the vet conceded. 'Give it more time to settle down.' And he made it quite clear our appointment was over.

So, reluctantly, I took Rocky home and allowed more time to go by, but of course, nothing changed.

Back and forth we went to the vet's but still no problem could be found. In the end, I remembered my old Irish vet who was now working a three-hour drive away. At least he understood me and the way my strange insights could be relied on as accurate, even if he couldn't figure out how I came by them. He'd discovered this by chance a few years before when he'd taken a blood test from my previous dog, Porsche, and diagnosed leukaemia.

'I don't think so,' I said, 'I think she needs an operation. I think she's got ladies' problems. Gynaecological.'

Thank goodness he decided to listen to me. It turned out Porsche had endometriosis, and an operation to remove the problem sorted her out in record time. She didn't have leukaemia at all. From then on, the vet took my suggestions seriously.

So now there was only one thing for it. I had to go back to the man who was prepared to listen to me. Some people might have thought I was crazy, but I tucked Rocky up in the car and set off across the country to my old vet's surgery, three hours away.

Thank goodness for an open-minded professional!

'I trust your instincts Diane!' said the vet when I explained the problem. 'Rocky's basically in good health. We'll put him under anaesthetic and check out those gums.'

Sure enough, when I went back to collect Rocky after his op, it turned out that several painful pieces of tooth had been left buried in his gum. No wonder he looked so miserable. My old vet removed them, stitched up the gum and within the week Rocky was tucking into his food with his old enthusiasm.

I was so happy to have my cheerful little dog back. If only all medical professionals could be a bit more open-minded, I thought again.

I did give the first vet an update on Rocky's condition, but to be honest he didn't seem particularly interested.

It's rather disconcerting but sometimes I get unexpected insights about people too. I remember one young woman, who came to see me at my office, keen to contact her dad. She'd been very close to her dad and missed him badly. She wanted to know he was okay, and that he was still nearby.

Young and bubbly with a beautiful mane of glossy dark brown hair and a brilliant smile, she sat down eagerly, mystified by the process as most new clients are, but keen to hear what I had to say.

As usual, after exchanging a few words, I turned away from the young woman and stared at the blank wall waiting for the pictures that would reveal her world. It didn't take long. Soon information about her dad and the family came flooding through and the young woman was very pleased.

Yet after a while, the atmosphere in the room seemed to change. I kept being shown images of a hospital and medical instruments. Could it be something to do with her dad? I wondered. Or maybe her mum. But no. My guide stepped in and indicated I must look into the young woman's own physical condition. It was very important.

I glanced round at her, still leaning forward eagerly on her chair, young and glowing, the picture of good health. I couldn't believe there was anything wrong with her, yet my guide was insistent.

I glanced back at the wall. Now a picture of the young woman herself appeared, and it was as if I could see right inside her body. I could make out small speckles of black inside her. Not a good sign, I knew. Cancer is often shown to me in this way. But she was so young and she looked so well…

'Now don't worry,' I said, 'but they're telling me you must get a medical check-up very soon. It's very important. Have you had any checks recently?'

The young woman looked a bit guilty. 'Well to be honest I'm s'posed to have had a smear test – well ages ago – but I didn't go. I feel fine though. I'm not ill.'

'You look great,' I said, 'but they're still saying you must get checked out as soon as possible. Everything will be fine, but you need to go for that check, *now*.'

It wasn't the best way to end a reading. I didn't want to frighten her, but I knew it was vital she saw a doctor urgently.

Thank goodness she took my advice. A few weeks later she phoned me back. 'Diane you saved my life!' she said, 'It was cervical cancer – the early stages. They caught it just in time. If it hadn't been for you, I'd have had to have a major operation. I might even have died.'

Phew! I was so glad she'd come to see me when she did. If she'd missed the appointment or refused to take the warning seriously, she might well not be here today.

Sometimes I'm not even in working mode when these flashes come to me. I'll never forget, a few years ago, I was sunbathing in the garden with my best friend, Sue, when I noticed a mole on her leg. Sue often wore skirts so I must have seen her legs before and noticed the mole without realising it, but now my eyes could not stop staring at it. There was something very wrong about that mole, that's for sure.

'Sue, I think you should get the doctor to have a look at that mole,' I said.

'What, this?' Sue looked down at it, 'It's been there for ages. I don't think it's changed.'

'Well, cover it up from the sun now to be on the safe side,' I said, 'and do me a favour! Get the doctor to look at it.'

Sue probably thought I was being a fusspot but she knows

what I'm like so the following week she went to the doctor. Sure enough the mole turned out to be cancerous. It was swiftly removed and Sue's prompt action might have saved her life.

There are occasions too, when during a reading, I get a warning of health problems that haven't yet materialised – conditions that will develop – often quite a long way in the future.

I was reminded of this one day, when I had a call from a lovely lady, called Cecelia. When I picked up the phone, this beautiful, educated voice curled out, almost like music – a voice I recognised, but couldn't quite place.

'Diane, you probably won't remember,' said Cecelia, 'but I came to see you a couple of years ago. You told me to call you if my daughter started getting headaches. I couldn't understand what you meant at the time as she was only a toddler and absolutely fine.'

'Well she's having headaches now. We took her for a brain scan and we've just been told she's got a brain tumour.'

'Oh, I am sorry Cecilia,' I said. As she was speaking, my mind was scrolling rapidly back through a number of clients, and suddenly a picture of a strikingly pretty little girl with shining black hair and brown eyes leapt onto the wall in front of me. Of course. Abigail.

It was quite a while ago now, but I recalled that during the reading, I'd been told that Cecelia's little daughter had been adopted from India because Cecelia was unable to have children.

Despite this, I had a strong feeling Cecelia would have her own biological baby one day – a little boy. 'And you will give him an unusual name, a name that means Prince,' I said.

Cecilia found this news hard to believe but she was pleased at the thought.

She and her husband were just thrilled to have been able to adopt the daughter they'd always wanted. Dozens of happy family scenes spilled out across the wall in front of me as I watched them playing with the bright, inquisitive child.

Yet the more I looked at the pictures of happy little Abigail, the more uneasy I felt. Something would go wrong with her head, I thought. Something inside. I didn't want to alarm Cecelia though. After all, Abigail was radiant with health right now, I didn't want to spoil things.

'Just call me in the future if Abigail ever starts getting headaches,' I said.

Cecilia's face fell. 'Should I be worried?'

'Oh no, no,' I said hastily. 'But she could possibly start getting headaches in years to come, and if she does, maybe I could help.'

Many months went by and I'd almost forgotten the incident, yet now here was Cecilia getting in touch again, just as I'd suggested, to confirm my worst fears.

'You said maybe you could help, Diane. D'you think you could come and give her some healing?'

'Yes of course,' I said.

Cecilia and her husband were so anxious to get the healing started right away, they insisted I should fly straight up from Wales to their home in London. They paid for tickets to the capital's City Airport and in record time I was off the plane and being met by Cecilia's husband Azam in a great big car. Soon we were bowling through the busy streets crammed with black taxi cabs and the famous scarlet double-decker buses.

It was a fine summer's day and London was looking its best. There seemed to be crowds of people everywhere, all brightly dressed. Tourists strolling, strung out across the pavements, business types zigzagging nimbly between them, and mixtures of the two sprawled in pavement cafés, enjoying the sunshine.

Amazing how many trees there are in London too, I found myself thinking, as we passed through another shady avenue lined with soaring London planes.

After a while, Azam turned into a leafy street in what looked to be one of the capital's more fashionable districts. Immediately the door to one of the houses was flung open and Cecilia and Abigail were standing there, (they must have been watching out for us) both cool and trim in white summer dresses.

Cecilia welcomed me into an elegant hall, all black and white floor tiles and huge vases of white lilies, and then on into an equally elegant sitting room. They had exquisite taste. Everywhere I looked, everything matched.

Little Abigail was chatting away cheerfully the whole time. No more than four years old she held a conversation like a child twice her age. She was clearly highly intelligent, and oddly, with her thick dark hair and cheeky smile she was the image of her dad – despite the fact he wasn't her biological father.

'We're going to go along with the treatment the hospital recommends,' Cecelia explained, 'but we'd be very grateful if you could give her healing as well.'

It seemed like a good plan to me. So Cecilia got Abigail to sit down – on the breakfast bar in the kitchen, as it happened, as Abigail insisted she wanted to see everything that was going on.

She didn't like me touching her head but I was able to hold my hands very close to her hair and let the healing energy flow through. I got a strong impression that the treatment was going to work, but it would take a couple of years and poor Abigail would have to go through a lot. Eventually she'd be fine though.

Unfortunately, I sensed there might be further issues to watch out for, a few years later, when she was around eleven.

Afterwards, I promised Cecilia that I could now continue

Abigail's healing from home, just by looking at a photograph of the child, combined with regular phone updates.

And that's what we did. Every evening, I took out Abigail's picture and visualised blue light beaming into her head and shrinking the tumour. And from time to time, I'd phone for updates. Often Abigail herself would answer the phone.

'Oh hello, Diane,' she'd say more like a sixteen-year-old than a little scrap of nearly 5. 'I knew it was you by your Welsh accent. How is life treating you?'

And I couldn't help chuckling. She was such a funny little thing.

The good news was, the tumour was shrinking, little by little. Abigail had some tough times to endure. She lost all her hair at one point and must have felt wretched, but her irrepressible personality ensured she didn't stay down for long. She was always bright and bubbly, and two years later she was back at school, fit, healthy and discovering a great talent for art.

'I'm going to be an architect when I grow up,' she told me proudly. 'Mummy says I can do anything I set my mind to do.'

There was more good news too. After all these years of being told she'd never have a child, Cecilia discovered she was pregnant. Just as I predicted the baby was a boy and they called him Raja – which apparently means 'Prince'.

It gives me so much pleasure to be able to help families in this way. It's always sad when someone is seriously ill, but when that sick person is also someone's much loved child – of whatever age – it's even more poignant.

The great thing about healing too, is that we can all contribute. We can all send out healing thoughts – you don't have to be a medium or a psychic to do your bit. I truly believe all healing prayers are helpful. The more the better.

So, when Shirley, a desperate mum got in touch with me about her badly injured son, lying at death's door in the hospital, I thought I'd ask my Facebook friends (these days I've got quite a few!) to join me in creating a huge wave of healing energy to send to the young man to help him pull through.

It was a terrible motorbike accident that had changed young James' life so tragically. Apparently, he hadn't long had this fabulous new machine, and he was eager to show it off to his best mate, Julian. That fateful night, the two of them roared off down the road on the gleaming new bike, enjoying every thrilling minute. James was an experienced motorcyclist and a good rider. Julian trusted him completely and neither dreamed that anything could go wrong. The weather was fine, visibility good and James knew the road well.

Suddenly, not far from home, something shot out in front of them, James was forced to swerve to avoid it, the bike skidded out of control and the two young men were flung violently into the road.

Julian was killed instantly, while James, barely breathing, was rushed to hospital in a coma.

'They say he probably won't live,' his distraught mum told me, 'but if he does, he'll be paralysed from the neck down.'

'Well don't give up on him,' I said gently. 'Let's see what I can pick up. Send me a photo of James and I'll do my best.'

Shortly afterwards the photo arrived. I stared down at the handsome young man looking up at me from the picture. Bright eyes full of hope for the future beamed out – completely unaware that in a few short months his whole life would come crashing down.

'And his girlfriend's having a baby soon,' said a woman's voice in my ear. 'A little girl it will be…'

Before I could ask any more questions, the speaker was elbowed aside and a male voice came in. 'I won't let him die,' he said. 'I'm helping him. He won't die.'

It was Julian. Though he'd only just arrived in the spirit world he was so determined to save his friend, he'd made a huge effort to get in contact. I expect my spirit guides were helping him because I suspect it's not easy for new souls to learn what to do at first.

'And he *will* walk again,' Julian went on, 'despite what the doctors say. He will walk again. I'll be helping him.'

Julian obviously bore his friend no animosity for the accident. He knew it was unavoidable and he still cared deeply for his mate.

'It's going to be tough for him, and it will take a good year,' Julian went on, 'but he *will* get on his feet again.'

That's what I needed to hear.

'Your boy will live,' I reassured Shirley, 'and one day he'll walk again but it'll take time. I'll send healing.'

As I spoke, I saw a quick picture of James sitting in a wheelchair, very much alive and working hard to stand up. Somehow, against all the odds, he was going to pull through.

That night, I started visualising sending blue light into the unconscious figure, all hooked up to wires and machines in the quiet little hospital room. I also put out an appeal to my friends on Facebook, asking them to send healing thoughts or prayers to the tragic young man. So many of them responded immediately, saying that they'd do everything they could to help. Healing energy must have been pouring invisibly into that young man's room from all over the country, maybe from overseas too, for hours on end. How could all that love directed towards him be anything other than good?

Night after night we repeated the healing, and finally Shirley got in contact with the wonderful news – James had survived and he'd woken up!

The doctors still thought he'd be paralysed and warned Shirley that her son must prepare himself for life in a wheelchair, but at least he'd cleared the first hurdle. He was back in the land of the living.

Over the following months, Shirley kept in touch. James was fighting hard. He'd had a number of setbacks, but he battled through them all, and after eight months, he was getting about in a wheelchair and walking in physiotherapy, with the aid of some special equipment on his legs.

What's more, his girlfriend had given birth to a beautiful baby girl, so James was now a proud dad as well. One more reason to go on fighting. I'm quite sure it won't be long before he's back on his feet unaided.

Of course Julian was doing his bit from the spirit world, but I'm convinced the combined power of all those healing prayers made the crucial difference for James.

Twelve

Coming out of the dentist's one afternoon, nursing a very sore jaw, I decided to treat myself to a magazine to cheer myself up.

I could hardly believe it. Somehow I'd ended up with a dental problem very similar to Rocky's and just a few months later, at that! Only in my case, in extracting my deeply rooted tooth - which was quite a struggle, to be fair - the dentist had managed to crack my jaw. What's more, just as in Rocky's case, the injury, though agony, wasn't obvious to the naked eye, and just like Rocky's vet, the dentist was highly sceptical of my own diagnosis. Even more so when I told him the reason I was so convinced I was right. Talk about deja-vu all over again!

'Psychic!' said the dentist, trying, not completely successfully, to keep the sarcasm out of his voice. 'You know this about your jaw… because… you're psychic…'

'That's right,' I said, but I could see he didn't believe me.

I sighed. The only way to convince him was to prove it, I realised. So I made myself more comfortable in the big black surgery chair, relaxed my shoulders and let my mind reach out towards him, and also his loved ones in spirit. Soon, interesting details about his divorce, his family and the things he'd been up to recently began to float into my thoughts and I started reeling them off, out loud.

'Oh my goodness!' cried the dentist in astonishment, as he recognised the juicy titbits I was describing. He even went a little pale as they began to mount up, 'You *are* psychic, aren't you!'

He seemed quite stunned and maybe he wanted me to stop,

too, before I discovered anything else!

'Well okay,' he said, 'we'll do another X-ray, to set your mind at rest.'

And of course the X-ray revealed a crack in my jaw, just as I knew it would. No wonder the pain's kept me awake at night, I thought afterwards, as I left the surgery and collected my prescription. At least I knew I wasn't going crazy. I crossed the road and popped into the newsagent's opposite. It would be good to get home, put my feet up and relax with a warm drink and a light-hearted read, to take my mind off the whole sorry saga.

Inside the newsagent's, shelves of brightly coloured magazines marched down the whole of one wall from floor to ceiling. There were so many it was almost confusing. So difficult to choose. I began to walk slowly down the display, trying to take them all in. Then my eye fell on one that seemed to jump out from all the others. The cover featured the most beautiful picture of Kate, or Catherine as we call her now, the Duchess of Cambridge, her glorious chestnut hair cascading round her shoulders, a warm, friendly smile on her face.

That's the one, I thought, lifting it down from the shelf, I would enjoy reading about that wholesome young Royal couple and looking at all the glossy photos. I started towards the till to pay, magazine in hand, but just as I turned, I sensed someone standing behind me.

'You see, I said she'd be perfect, didn't I?' said Princess Diana's voice in my ear.

I recognised her voice immediately. I couldn't see her but I knew she was there, admiring the magazine cover over my shoulder.

Princess Diana! It had been a long time since I'd heard from her. 'You certainly did,' I replied inwardly.

Instantly my mind flew back several years. It was not long after I'd won Britain's Psychic Challenge. A great many requests were coming in, asking me to take part in all manner of psychic feats. I couldn't possibly agree to them all, but one in particular stood out.

An American TV company was making a documentary about the Royals. Would it be possible, they asked, for me to come to London and do a psychic prediction, on camera, about Prince William and his then girlfriend, Kate Middleton? What did I see ahead for them as a couple? Were they going to get married? And if so, what would their wedding be like?

I've always been a fan of the Royal Family, particularly Princess Diana, so I was thrilled. I'd be interested to know the answers to those documentary questions myself!

'Of course,' I told the producer. It would be so intriguing to see what I could come up with.

A few days later, there I was, on the train, bright and early, and dressed in my most colourful clothes for the camera, as requested, speeding through the Welsh countryside, towards Paddington Station.

By now, I'd done so much TV work that I was more excited than nervous. All the same, I like to prepare ahead if possible, just in case the hurly-burly of the studio should make psychic contact more difficult. The carriage wasn't too crowded at that point, so I leaned back against my padded seat, half closed my eyes, and concentrated on reaching Princess Diana – or Lady Diana as I always thought of her.

After a moment or two, the sights and sounds of the swaying train receded into the background and Diana's beaming face, her blonde hair fluffed round her features like a halo, floated into my mind. She looked very happy.

'So what do you think of William's girlfriend, Kate Middleton?' I asked her inwardly.

'She's perfect,' said Diana immediately. 'The perfect wife for my handsome son. I'm so pleased. Yes of course they'll get married. And I'll be there at their wedding. I'm going to wear a pastel pink suit!'

Wow! What a shame the whole world won't be able to see you, I thought to myself.

'Will it be a good marriage?' I asked. After all, Diana, and William's Dad, Prince Charles, hadn't been too lucky in that department.

'Yes,' said Diana firmly, 'she'll make him very happy. She's the right one for my William. It was love at first sight you know. They'd been sweethearts since 2001. Now, they do everything together. They both like the same things and William doesn't mind doing his share and getting stuck into the cooking.'

'Where will they live?' I wondered.

'Really, they'd love a farm of their own – a place where they can bring up a family surrounded by nature,' said Diana. 'They're very into organic food and the countryside. All natural things. They're going to have three beautiful children, and William will make a great dad. I can see him helping the little ones to dress in the mornings and making their breakfast.'

Back then, it was still early in the couple's relationship, and the things Diana was talking about were a long way in the future. The TV company would probably like something a bit more immediate, I thought, so: 'What about now?' I asked silently. 'What's going to happen next?'

'They're going to live in Wales,' said Diana. 'Their first home will be like a farmhouse, with a big pine table in the kitchen. They'll be happy there.'

Then she went on to describe their wedding. She explained it would be a lovely day and Kate would look perfect in a slim-fitting gown that accentuated her slender figure, and she'd wear her hair loose and natural round her shoulders, the way William loves to see it.

Obviously, at the time, there was no way of knowing if this

information was right or wrong, but presumably the TV producers wouldn't mind.

'Thank you. That's very helpful,' I told Diana gratefully. I'd have plenty to talk about on the TV show now, I thought.

I sat up straighter and let the Diana link slip quietly away, while the sounds of the carriage slowly returned. Then suddenly, just as the princess had almost gone, she sent one last, strange picture swimming into my mind. It was William and Kate, both dressed in what looked like space suits.

How peculiar, I thought, as the impression dissolved. I got a strong feeling that the couple were very interested in space exploration, as well as ecology.

Could it be that one day they'd actually take a flight into space? I wondered. Or perhaps simply visit an astronaut training centre and try out some of the exercises? Only time would tell but I wouldn't be a bit surprised.

Oddly enough, that interview with the TV company wasn't my first encounter with Princess Diana. I'd been an admirer ever since her shy, Lady Di days. After all, we shared the same name and were similar ages, but also, I recognised that glowing, spiritual quality that shone through her. She was clearly a very special lady.

I was so sad when she died, though I had the oddest feeling, she knew it was going to happen. Not so much that she would be killed in a car crash perhaps, but more that she sensed she would die young.

Then, a few months after her funeral, I had the most incredible dream. It was so vivid and so detailed, I believe I actually visited her in the spirit world, during my sleep. Or maybe she visited me and took me to some sort of halfway house, between our two worlds.

At any rate, wherever it was, the two of us were in a beautiful room. There was a big fireplace in front of us and an old fashioned green velvet sofa, with sprays of flowers across the fabric, and chunky scroll arms. But we weren't sitting on the sofa, we were sitting side by side on the floor.

Diana was dressed in stretchy light blue pants, with a tee-shirt in identical blue, that matched her eyes. It looked as if she was just back from the gym. There she was, crossed-legged on the carpet next to me, close enough to touch, and we were deep in conversation about the work I do.

For some reason, now I could see that she was wearing a lot of jewellery: bracelets on her wrists, glittering chains around her neck. Yet they didn't look particularly expensive. She took one off and handed it to me.

'These mean nothing to me. Nothing at all,' she said. 'Happiness is what counts. Happiness and love. Keep on doing what you're doing Diane. What you do is special. Look at this. Look and learn.'

She swept her arm towards me and suddenly I was looking at a vision of a huge football stadium, packed with thousands and thousands of people. They were even sitting all across the pitch.

'Watch the ones who stand up,' said Diana. 'They are the only truly gifted people in the world.'

As I watched, an elderly woman stood up, then a foreign looking gentleman, then another couple of people… but they were so few amongst that vast crowd.

'And you're going to be there too,' said Diana. 'You're special. You're going to do so much for charity, and to help other people. I was there as well. I died for a reason, you know. Dodi and I had big plans, but it wasn't to be. I was needed, to help others from behind the scenes. I'm carrying on from over here.

But of course I will always look after my boys, no matter what. I want them to know how much I love them.'

She stood up. 'I've got to go now,' she said moving towards

the door, 'but well done Diane. I'll see you soon.'

And then she was gone. I woke up to find the sun was already sliding through a gap in the curtains, filling the room with golden light. Wow, I thought, laying back against the pillows. Just wow! And a sense of wonder stayed with me all day.

Thirteen

What is it with all this computer dating? I was thinking to myself one night. There I was, sitting watching TV, dinner on my knee, Rocky curled up contentedly beside me. I was all alone – apart from Rocky, of course - but perfectly happy in my own company. After a long day in the office I was tired, in a good way, and glad just to relax, watch something undemanding, and not have to worry about anyone else.

But several of my friends were going crazy about a particular dating site and reckoned I should give it a try. After all, I'd been single for years now. They thought it was time I had some romance in my life.

'Come on Di,' coaxed my friend Jay. 'You deserve some fun.'

Jay's experiences with the site had been mixed, to say the least. Some of the men she'd met looked nothing like their photos. One was about twenty years older than the age he'd put down; others told massive fibs about their occupations. Amazing how many 'pilots' and 'company directors' turned out to be unemployed!

Yet Jay had also met some very interesting characters and I loved hearing about her adventures. Despite this, I still hesitated about signing up myself, even though it was free.

Then a woman from Greece contacted me, with an unusual request. She divided her time between her home in Greece, and a place in London, she explained, and she was looking for a husband online. So far though, she'd had no luck with the men she'd picked herself. All duds one way or another, she explained, so she wondered if I could use my psychic powers to check the candidates out and find someone genuine for her.

Trouble was, this lady was quite particular. She wanted a man who was a similar age to herself, had a similar amount of wealth, plus he must be slim, with a good, thick head of hair, and blue eyes. Oh… and he mustn't be shorter than she was either.

It wasn't going to be easy, I could see that, but matchmaking's fun and if I could find her the perfect man, I'd be thrilled, I thought. So I agreed. Soon she was sending me photos of various gentlemen she found appealing.

'This man tells me he's a pilot, he's got money and he lives in London,' she'd write beneath the image of some attractive silver-fox. 'Do you think that's correct?'

I'd stare at the manly smile and crinkly blue eyes and invariably a big 'No way!' would leap into my mind.

'He's a warehouseman from Slough and he's broke!' a waspish voice told me on one occasion. 'That's not even his photo. He copied that from the internet. The man there's an actor from Michigan!'

To be fair, many of the prospective dates were genuinely looking for love, but somehow I couldn't seem to find anyone suitable for my Greek client.

'Maybe you could join the site yourself,' she suggested, 'and then you'd be able to see the new pictures straight away as they come up.'

As it happened, my friends Karen and Julie had the same idea. Both keen online dating fans, they thought it would be perfect if I could check out the prospective partners that came up for them, and screen out any that were not being entirely honest, or whose boyish grins concealed a nasty temper.

I have to admit that, by now, I was intrigued to see for myself what they were all on about, so in the end I filled in the online form. I didn't include a photograph though. I didn't say I was a psychic, either. After all, I wasn't looking for a partner for myself – this was purely research.

The strange thing was, as I scrolled through the large pictures of various men who might interest my Greek client, or one of my girlfriends, I noticed a string of additional, miniature portraits of other site members, flying by across the bottom of the screen.

One in particular seemed to jump out. The man had very dark hair, blue, blue eyes and a blue shirt. Just looking at the tiny photo, I felt a strange pull towards him.

'He's my grandson,' said a woman's voice in my ear. 'He's a really funny guy.'

She sounded so proud, I pulled up the man's profile to take a closer look – strictly out of curiosity you understand! His name was Dean, I read, and he was single, but he lived way off in the West Midlands. Much too far from Wales to be practical for meeting up.

I minimised the profile again. What a shame, I thought. He looked so nice. Still, I wasn't looking for a man for myself anyway. What was I thinking? And I went back to my search for the others.

Yet an odd thing happened. Every time I logged onto the site for my friends, the same little string of pictures would be spooling across the foot of the screen, and Dean, of the blue eyes and blue shirt, would capture my attention, in a way that was becoming disconcerting.

I couldn't help mentioning it to the girls when we met for occasional nights out.

'Message him!' said Jay.

'Yes, contact him!' encouraged Julie. 'What harm could it do? You're always telling us to trust our gut feelings. What have you got to lose? Just see what he says. He might not even acknowledge you.'

Unseen by anyone else, a woman called Margaret was also turning up at my side, at regular intervals, telling me what a nice man this Dean was and how well we'd get on.

So what could I do? I contacted him! But I kept my message brief.

'What a shame you live so far away,' I wrote. 'I know you're a really funny guy. Take care. Diane.'

Short and sweet! But within minutes, Dean answered.

'Where are you from?' he asked. 'And I can't see a photograph of you. Hey, where do you actually live?'

I explained that I lived in a small village, just outside Swansea in Wales. I also told him I was a magazine columnist – which was true at the time, but not the whole truth. At that point I had a psychic agony column in 'That's Life' magazine. It wasn't my main job but I didn't want him to think I was weird at this stage! I also sent him a photo.

Dean explained he'd been in the Army, then worked as a gas engineer, before joining his father's engineering business. He loved Wales, he said, especially Tenby where he'd spent a lot of time when he was in the Army. Oh and he loved the photo!

For the next few nights we couldn't stop chatting online. We seemed to have so much in common that, in the end, Dean said he'd like to come and meet me in person.

'You know I wouldn't normally drive to the other side of Birmingham to meet someone,' he laughed, 'and now here I am coming all the way to Swansea for a date!'

I was a bit nervous of course. I couldn't remember the last time I'd been on a date. I felt like I was sixteen again, with tickly butterflies in my tummy. Yet every instinct was telling me the evening would go well.

And it did. We went to a lovely restaurant in the Mumbles – the picturesque peninsula that stretches out into the sea, at the far end of Swansea. Even more famous now as it featured quite a bit in the hit TV series, 'Gavin and Stacey'.

Dean turned out to be as handsome as his photo. Tall, and dark, with those amazing blue eyes and very broad shoulders.

As soon as I saw him, some long-forgotten words of my old student, Mike, flew into my mind. Mike was practising his clairvoyance one evening, when out of nowhere he said he had a message for me:

'There's going to be another man in your life,' said Mike slowly, 'and he's got very big shoulders!'

I'd laughed at the time. It seemed so unlikely, and such an odd description. Of all the things you might notice about a person, how odd that it should be his shoulders. But standing here, after all these years, looking at my date, there was no denying Dean had very big shoulders!

In the restaurant, we were given one of the best window seats, looking out across the bay, and over a glass of wine, we both ended up choosing more or less the same meal: scallops to start, then steak (with chips for him and with salad for me) and we both finished with crème brulee for dessert. Best of all, we laughed and laughed the whole evening and we didn't stop talking. We really did get on like a house on fire.

Despite us living so far apart, it was quite obvious we were going to meet again. And so without even intending it, after all these years of being single, I ended up in a relationship – albeit a long distance relationship. It was so easy being around Dean. He was always cheerful and happy, and made me laugh all day long.

Though as we grew closer, I found myself feeling puzzled and a bit troubled. I'd been so certain Peter was my soulmate, but now Dean seemed so right and he made me so happy. As if he was my soulmate too. How could this be?

I had to admit, I still had complicated feelings for Peter. Although the romance between us was gone, I still cared deeply for him. There was a bond between us that I sensed could never be broken. In fact, I often had a strange recurring dream that was more like a glimpse of some past life together.

I could see the two of us, little Peter and I, as kids, living on the streets of London. It must have been centuries ago because the streets were cobbled and oil lanterns flickered in the windows of the houses as we passed. We were dressed in rags, holding hands and running, just running and giggling.

Then we dashed by an old woman. She was wearing a long dress that dragged on the stones, and her hair was hidden by a hat with feathers on.

'You look like a lovely lady!' I called cheekily over my shoulder, as we skipped by. 'I like your hat.'

She stopped and looked at me. 'Come here child,' she said.

So, a little warily, I went back and moved closer, to see what she wanted. To my surprise, she opened the little drawstring bag she was carrying, and with one neat, gloved hand, she took out a tiny coin and gave it to me.

Thrilled, I thanked her and then Peter and I dashed off again and used the coin to buy an apple from a market stall. I'm not sure if I was older than Peter; we were both very small, but it was clear I looked after him. I was the stronger, bolder one of us and I gave him half my apple!

There was something so vivid and real about this scene that I'm quite sure it actually happened. I believe we'd been together in the past. Maybe more than once. So if we were destined to meet again in the 21st century, why hadn't we stayed together today?

It was baffling. Then one evening the answer came to me. Maybe it was Florence who put the idea in my head – after all, she should know!

I realised we've always been led to believe that each one of us has a single soulmate in life. A special 'one-and-only' it's our romantic mission to find. But suddenly it seemed to me this notion wasn't quite right. Supposing we did in fact have several soulmates – partners who've been sent to join us at just the right moment on our journey to help us with a particular part of our development, and then, when their task is complete, they move on?

For some people, the lessons they have to teach each other can last a whole lifetime, so these couples are the ones that 'death us do part'. But others require a series of different 'teachers' as their lives progress, so these are the people who embark on a number of relationships, each precious and valuable in its own very important way. Each appropriate to a particular phase of their life.

Peter, I realised, had been very good for me at a particular time. He was a wonderful father to my children and he gave me the confidence I so badly needed to make the most of myself.

I've always been dyslexic, and went to school at a time when very little was known about the condition, so I grew up always feeling a bit inferior as far as book learning is concerned. In the company of intellectual types, I'd get tongue-tied and hardly dared say a word, in case I showed my ignorance. But Peter insisted on taking me out and about with his barrister and QC friends, and encouraged me to speak up and air my views in front of these highly-educated people.

'You're just as intelligent as them,' he'd assure me, 'more intelligent than most of them in fact!'

He valued my psychic perception and the way I could sum up whoever I met in an instant. Often, he'd ask my opinion about clients or cases he was working on, and I was usually right. He even took me to court with him at times so I could observe and advise him on what was really going through the judges' mind as the case progressed.

Peter taught me to be proud of my psychic abilities. They were enormously useful, he assured me.

Before I met him, I'd never really analysed the effect my

childhood must have had on me, but during all the years I was growing up, I was either scolded for telling fibs, or shushed from speaking out about the impossible things I just 'knew', for fear of people thinking I was strange or mad.

'You mustn't mention spirits,' Mum would insist. 'People'll think there's something wrong with you.'

No wonder, by the time I was an adult, it was second nature to me to keep quiet about my gift, until I really knew someone would understand. I wasn't exactly ashamed of my powers, I just didn't want people to think I was crazy, or alternatively, a bit frightening, like some sort of witch.

Thank goodness for Peter getting me over all that. He didn't think I was a freak and in fact, he was proud of my powers.

'You can be ahead of everyone,' he used to say. 'For goodness sake you can even call on your spirit guides to teach you how to do things. You picked up golf in record time!' – Peter was a keen golfer – 'The possibilities are endless!'

He was so impressed with my gift that he used to tell everyone about the amazing things I could do. In fact, sometimes his enthusiasm got me into embarrassing situations.

Early in our relationship, I ran a tearoom in the village – something I'd always wanted to do. Anyway, one busy Friday morning, a scruffy-looking man walked in, with a pile of books under his arm.

I was in the kitchen, making a fresh batch of Welsh cakes, when Linda, our waitress, popped her head round the door.

'There's a man out there, got some books for you,' she said. 'Says he's a client of your husband's.'

Puzzled, I walked through to the tearoom. There he was, standing by the dresser. A big man in a rumpled coat, with a purple-red face, like a farmer who'd spent too long on the hills in all weathers. Then suddenly, all around him I glimpsed a bottle green aura – poison green – radiating out from all around his frame like some sort of diabolical outline. The second my eyes met his, it was like I'd been punched in the stomach. My insides clenched violently and I thought I might be sick.

'I've just been talking to your husband,' said the man, completely unaware of my horrified reaction.

'He tells me you're a psychic. I'm really into all that stuff. Mediums and such. I thought you might find some of my books interesting. There's all sorts here: psychic ability, healing, crystals... you name it, I've got it. Have a read. I'd be interested to know what you think.'

There was no way I could touch the books he was holding out. I couldn't have taken anything from those poisonous hands if he'd been holding out a cheque for a million pounds.

Fortunately, my own hands were still covered in flour.

'Oops, sorry!' I said, holding up my dusty white fingers. 'Our waitress will take them. Many thanks. Most thoughtful.'

Linda obligingly took the books from him and put them on the shelf.

The man smiled. 'Let me know when you've finished with them. I've got to come back and see your husband again anyway. No rush.'

And then he was gone. I sighed with relief. My stomach began to relax and the nauseous feeling faded. There was something very wrong about that man, I thought, as I went back to the kitchen – you dropped me right in it there, Peter!

A few weeks went by. Linda put the books away in a cupboard out of sight, and I'd almost forgotten the incident when, one day, a woman came in.

'Hi. You don't know me,' she said, 'but my neighbour's asked me to collect some books for him. He left you some books on healing and psychic things? Could I take them back for him?'

'Of course!' I said gratefully. I'd be glad to get rid of them.

Linda hurried off to find them in the cupboard, and while she waited, the woman shuffled a bit awkwardly between the tables.

'He's a very nice man, my neighbour,' she said, 'but... well... between you and me, he's up in court tomorrow. His wife's accused him of child abuse. His daughters say he sexually abused them. That can't be right, surely? Do you think it's true, Diane? I mean, he seems so nice...'

So that explains it, I thought. He's an abuser. Thanks a lot Peter – sending him to me! I couldn't voice my opinion about the man out loud, of course. He hadn't even been found guilty yet.

'Oh, well...' I struggled for an enigmatic reply, 'I... er... oh, and here's Linda with the books!'

I beamed in relief as our waitress hurried towards us with a bulging carrier bag in her arms. She handed it to the woman.

'There you are,' I said. 'Thanks for picking them up. Sorry, must go. I've got some scones in the oven.'

I wasn't really annoyed with Peter for sending the man to me of course. I knew he was simply so proud of what I could do, he couldn't help talking about it. I should be grateful. Some husbands might be resentful of the attention I attracted.

We were so good for each other in those early years, I couldn't imagine how the relationship could change. Though, oddly, I was often aware of my Grandfather warning cryptically at the back of my mind: 'It won't last forever you know. You'll feel let down.'

I refused to believe it. He was being pessimistic, I told myself. Peter was my soulmate. I couldn't imagine why I'd feel let down.

I'd come across quite a few women who felt let down by their husbands, during the course of my work, and most of them had good reason to feel that way – on account of the fact their man was cheating on them with someone else. But Peter wasn't like that. I trusted him completely.

But a few years later, along came the recession with its devastating effects on our relationship. Suddenly Peter was in Dubai, I was picking up the pieces in Wales, and *yes*, I did feel all alone and let down. As usual Grandfather was right.

Despite the problems though, I believe Peter and I will never be completely apart because we've been together in many different ways in many different lifetimes.

It's strange, really. I'd never thought much about past lives until they started cropping up in my readings.

The first time it happened, I was in my office working with a thoroughly modern lady. There she was, sitting calmly, opposite me, in her stylish trousers and smart jacket, chunky designer bag on the floor by her feet.

Yet when I looked at the wall, I kept seeing the same woman dressed in a billowing crinoline, curls bobbing round her neck as she ran, panicking, through a house full of candles. Smoke was seeping through the room behind her and it looked as if this poor lady was caught in a house fire.

Thankfully, as I watched, she reached a small side door, threw it open and burst out into the garden, to safety. But then she could only stand there looking on helplessly, as the flames shot through the roof and the whole building burned to the ground.

I sensed a dread of fire within her that persisted to this day. 'I think you have a massive fear of fires,' I began slowly.

'Yes I do, Diane,' she agreed, surprised. 'Why is that d'you think? I mean I even keep dreaming of fires.'

That was fortunate, I thought. My words wouldn't sound so unbelievable if she was already getting hints of the truth.

'It's because of what happened in your past life,' I explained.

'I can actually see that you were in a house, there was a fire but you managed to get out safely through a side door. The whole place burnt down though.'

'Oh my God!' said the woman, astonished, 'That's the dream I've always had. I could always see myself getting out of a small, old-fashioned house with a wooden door, while the whole place was on fire. I've been having that dream ever since I was a child. And I'm terrified of fires.'

So from that moment on, even though a lot of people don't believe it, I started to realise that most of us have probably lived before, and sometimes during a reading I could get a glimpse of what happened to a client in the past. It was fascinating to see how events back then could, at times, echo down the centuries and somehow affect the client in the present. Maybe that explains so-called irrational fears, such as the horror of confined spaces, or heights or water, or any other phobia that seems to strike out of nowhere. I mean, if you drowned in a past life, it would be understandable if you ended up with a fear of water in the present.

I don't know that I can call up someone's past life at will, it just seems to happen spontaneously during a reading, but when it occurs, it's just like watching a historical film – a costume drama unfolding on my wall. What's more, when the client researches later, tiny details from the period that neither of us know anything about, turn out to be correct.

One lady who came to my office, turned out to be a man in a past life, and when I went on to describe the gentleman I could see her as, she didn't seem at all phased.

'Well, I never said, Diane,' she told me, 'but I'm gay and I've always felt more like a man than a woman.'

On another occasion, I found myself watching the long-ago life of my current client. Back then I heard her being called 'Anna... for short,' so her real name must have been Annabel perhaps, or something similar. Anna was sad because it turned out she couldn't have children and she eventually passed away from some blood disorder that made her very tired.

'How strange,' said the woman afterwards. 'My middle name's Ann, and though I've got children, it was only thanks to IVF. What's more, since the babies were born I've tended to be anaemic – my blood isn't as good as it could be and I *do* get so tired at times.'

How strange, but endlessly fascinating, I thought. So the idea that Peter and I were together in a past life was possibly perfectly logical after all.

I've heard a theory that we're all part of 'soul groups,' that stick together in various different combinations throughout numerous lives, to help each other with whatever lessons we need to learn on Earth. Apparently, members of the group even agree, before they're born, what role they will play in the next life. So someone who was your father in one life, might end up being your brother or sister, your best friend, or maybe even your boss, in another life. That might explain why some people we just 'click with' instantly, while others we loathe on sight, for no fathomable reason.

Who knows, if that theory is correct, maybe Dean and I also knew each other at some distant point centuries ago, and decided to spend part of our new 21st century journey together once again.

Fourteen

I couldn't believe it. Christmas had come round again. The festive lights were going up all over Swansea, and carols were blasting from the radio. Time seemed to have speeded up since I met Dean – or maybe it was just because I'd got a new interest in life. It had been so long since I'd had anything to think about, besides my work, my kids and the rest of the family. I was feeling a bit like a giddy teenager.

'Why don't you come to Christmas lunch?' I asked Dean, impulsively, on the phone one day. 'It's always a good laugh and you could meet the family.'

It was only afterwards I realised how daunting that idea could seem to some men, but bless him, not to Dean.

'Love to,' said Dean immediately. He didn't need any persuading at all. He really was a friendly, gregarious soul.

Soon I was happily knee-deep in decorations, shopping lists and turkey orders. It's hard work but I adore all the fun and colour of the festive season, and this year was going to be even more exciting than usual because it was my first Christmas with Dean.

I was working until just a few days before the holiday, but for some reason as I left the office one frosty evening I decided to phone Dean to see how he was getting on with his preparations for the trip to Wales.

'Diane, I'm not supposed to be coming for days yet!' He laughed. 'I'm not getting ready till the weekend at least!'

But at the sound of his voice, a picture leapt instantly into my mind. Crystal clear, I could see Dean standing behind his black convertible car, trying to load a great big parcel awkwardly into the back.

At this point in our relationship, though he was always respectful, I knew Dean was sceptical about my psychic gift. He hadn't had anything to do with psychics before and he'd not yet seen me work, so it's hardly surprising he didn't really understand what I did. Even so, I couldn't help myself.

'Dean I've been doing readings today and I'm still in the zone,' I said. 'Right now, I can see you putting a big parcel into your car.'

'Oh really?' said Dean, trying to stifle a laugh.

'Yes really!' I went on. 'I can see you trying to put this great big parcel in the back. It's huge. You're going to have to take the roof off to fit that in. Dean – I think you've got me a TV for Christmas!'

He was really laughing now, but he wouldn't say.

'Oh, and I can see another parcel too!' I went on, as a bright, glittery object on the back seat suddenly caught my eye. 'Something sparkly, like a sort of cushion. Is it a sparkly cushion?'

Dean laughed even more. 'Stop it Diane!' he said teasingly. 'You're just going to have to wait and see.'

Well, Christmas Eve arrived, Dean drew up outside, and there, sticking up in the back of the car, I could plainly see a huge parcel all wrapped in jolly paper.

'My new TV!' I thought to myself, happily, but of course I didn't say.

Sure enough, Christmas morning, I opened my largest parcel to find a beautiful TV inside. The next gift was smaller and felt a little squishy. Carefully, I pulled off the sellotape and drew back the paper, to reveal a sparkly scarlet cover for my Ipad.

So that's what I'd seen on the back seat that looked like a cushion. A cover for my old iPad.

'It's perfect!' I said to Dean – exactly the kind of cover I'd have chosen myself, and it smartened up my iPad no end.

'I couldn't believe it,' Dean confessed, as he watched me collecting up the heap of torn wrappings later. 'When you phoned that night, I was actually in the car park with my brother-in-law, trying to load the great big TV box into the back of the car. And the iPad cover was on the seat. You certainly proved to me you're psychic. There's absolutely no way you could have known. Tell you what though. You didn't mention the bottle of perfume I bought you as well!'

'Didn't want to scare you too much,' I giggled. 'You might have changed your mind about coming!'

It was a great Christmas. Dean met my mum and step-dad, Don, and my big brother, Gary. They all liked him, but he and Gary got on especially well. They'd both been in the Army, though at different times, and the two of them had so much in common. Dean was fascinated to hear about Gary's experiences in the Falkland War days and Gary was interested to hear about the changes that had been made by the time Dean joined up.

Watching the two of them chatting away across the table, Gary so animated, I could see my brother was reliving, in his mind, the time he'd first strode out onto the parade ground, so proud, in his freshly pressed khaki uniform and clumpy boots so shiny you could see your face in them. He was only sixteen when he enlisted. No wonder our mum was worried to death.

When the Falklands War started and Gary was sent out there, I used to arrive home from school to find Mum sitting in front of the TV crying, as the latest reports from the battlefield came on the news. Every single night she was drawn compulsively to that screen, even though it upset her so much.

Machine gun fire and terrible explosions kept thundering into the living room, and every now and then, the night sky on screen would split open with another blinding bomb blast. We saw soldiers scurrying about, through dark, shadowy terrain, dodging bullets, and listened to terrified-looking reporters, nervously describing the latest battle, followed by grim updates on the casualties. Mum could hardly bear to watch, yet she couldn't stop herself.

'Why don't you turn it off?' I'd beg. 'It only scares you.'

'I can't Diane,' Mum would wail. 'I have to know what's happening.'

'But he'll be alright, Mum,' I insisted. 'Stop worrying yourself sick. He's coming home.'

I knew this for certain. One night as I lay in bed, praying to the angels to keep Gary safe, Grandfather appeared at the end of the bed. 'Don't worry,' he said reassuringly, 'we're looking after Gary. Your brother will be home safe and sound very soon. You'll see.'

I believed him completely. What's more, after that I kept seeing flashes of Gary in the future, back home and fit and strong as ever. There was Gary in his jeans and sweatshirt, walking upstairs. There was Gary out the front, looking at a car with his mates. There was Gary combing his hair in the mirror getting ready for a night out. Yes, Gary was definitely coming home.

But I couldn't expect Mum to take my word for it.

'You can't know, Diane!' she'd sniff, wiping her eyes with yet another damp tissue, 'But I hope you're right.'

And of course, thank heaven, Grandfather's words came true. Soon the great day came, when the war was over and we heard that Gary was coming home, uninjured.

Mum organised a monster banner that read: 'Welcome Home, Gary!' and had it draped across the front of the house; then she threw an exuberant party for him to celebrate.

It was a wonderful day, the day Gary came marching back.

But as he walked up the front path, I could see he'd come home a different man.

He was still our kind, dependable Gary but there was a new seriousness about him. He'd seen so much trauma. Men had been killed in action right in front of him, some of them his friends – you can't go through something like that and stay the same. No wonder he had nightmares. No wonder it took him a while to adjust.

Even so, no matter what he was going through inside, he was always patient and considerate with me. More like a dad than a brother, really. It meant a lot to me that he and Dean got on so well together.

But if the incident with the Christmas presents that year helped convince Dean about my psychic powers, he was to have good reason to be thankful for them a few years later. They probably saved his life!

I'd never met Dean's Uncle Mike, who sadly passed away quite young, with kidney problems, just before I had the chance to meet him. By all accounts, he was a lovely man. He and Dean were close, and he was delighted when he heard Dean was dating a Swansea girl, as Swansea was his favourite town, he always said.

Anyway, after a while, I noticed Dean seemed to be unusually tired when he came home from work. I knew he worked hard but there was something about this early evening exhaustion I felt sure wasn't right.

Typical man, Dean shrugged off my concern and said he felt fine, but I wasn't happy. I could sense his Uncle Mike hovering around him… and Uncle Mike was concerned.

'Get him checked out,' Uncle Mike said to me. 'Tell him to get his blood pressure checked, and his kidneys.'

I didn't want to nag but if Uncle Mike was bothered, as well as me, there must be something wrong. I couldn't help myself. I ended up politely pestering Dean almost every day to call the surgery.

'The only thing wrong is this weird thumping feeling in my back when I'm stressed,' Dean protested. 'But it goes off. It's nothing.'

What is it with men and doctors? Anyway in the end I wore him down and Dean eventually made an appointment with the doctor, only to get bogged down at work and forget to go. I couldn't believe it.

'Well make another appointment,' I begged, close to tears, 'and don't forget this time. It's important. Something awful could happen.'

So in the end Dean went to the doctor and got quite a shock.

The doctor took his blood pressure and almost recoiled in horror.

'By rights,' he said, 'I should send you to A&E right now. Your blood pressure is extremely high. This is not good at all. I need to put you on a monitor and start you on medication immediately. Then you're to go home and rest completely. If you feel unwell in any way, go straight to A&E. I'm also making an appointment for you for urgent tests at the hospital.'

Dean was astonished and mortified. He came home a little shame-faced. 'Looks like you were right Diane,' he agreed. 'I've got to take all these pills and go for more tests.'

It took weeks to get the problem sorted. It turned out Dean had an issue with his kidney, which accounted for the pain in his back when under stress, and this was causing his blood pressure to sky-rocket. He could have had a heart attack or stroke at any minute, he was told, which really shocked him.

Fortunately, the right medication restored him to health, and he was amazed how much better he felt.

'I must have been going downhill for months without even realising it,' he said later. 'I thought that tiredness was normal.

'You saved my life, I reckon, Diane.'

Another good reason for my gift, I thought happily.

Funnily enough that wasn't the first time I've been told I'd saved someone's life. Not long ago I got a note from a woman who'd listened to one of my meditation CDs. She said she'd been feeling suicidal, but after relaxing with my CD and following the guided meditation, she came to the end of the recording in a much happier frame of mind. In fact, now she was singing! I'd saved her life, she said.

It was wonderful to hear and wonderful to think my words could have such a powerful effect. Well, I say my words but really they're not mine, they come from the spirit world.

I was still running my meditation classes, with recordings for people who couldn't attend in person. I'd never had a lesson in meditation, it was just something I felt my Grandfather wanted me to do. I didn't really prepare anything in advance. I just took myself along to the hall, trusting that Grandfather or my guides would let me know what to do when the moment came. So I'd get everyone lying down, breathing deeply, relaxed and comfortable, then I said whatever the spirits told me to say. Occasionally, I'd look out across the resting forms and see spirit guides standing beside their particular person.

Sometimes I'd ask people to visualise their future. The results were amazing. Some people had difficulty visualising. I could tell just by looking at them, they found it a challenge to switch off, but others had miraculous results.

'My God, Diane,' one woman told me a couple of years later. 'In your class, I visualised my new husband. There was no way you could have known what he would have looked like. But he's exactly how I pictured him. I also visualised a new baby coming into the family, and two years later my daughter had a little girl.'

Another said, 'You asked me to visualise my future home, Diane. Well the house I saw is the house I've just moved into

– exactly as I envisioned it. Incredible.'

Others have listened to my healing CD, found they visualised themselves well, and actually experienced a great improvement in their condition. It's great to think that I don't even have to be there in person to help.

Not long after Dean and I started dating, a woman from the East Midlands, not far from Dean's area, contacted me. Mandy, her name was, and her heart was broken, she told me. She'd lost her young teenage son, Adam Jones, tragically killed in a hit and run incident. He was only 15, and the cowardly driver of the car that ran him down, had never been found.

'Can you help find my boy's killer Diane?' Mandy begged. 'The whole family's desperate.'

As she was speaking, a wave of tremendous energy swept through me and I caught a glimpse of a cheeky lad, with a chubby face, blond hair and a baseball cap on back to front. He grinned, unselfconsciously, in my direction and I could have sworn he winked. A real extrovert, that one, I thought to myself, smiling back. He had enormous charm – you could see it all over his face. Often up to mischief in his time no doubt, but you couldn't help loving him. This Adam Jones was clearly quite a character, and eager to chat.

'He's a real, lovable rogue,' I said to Mandy out loud. 'And a very strong communicator.'

Adam gave me a cheery thumbs up, then showed me a fleeting impression of the whole of him, the way his family usually saw him. He was eccentrically dressed, in a pair of shorts, teamed with sturdy wellington boots.

'That's right,' said Mandy when I described him. 'That's how he always went around, summer and winter, whatever the weather. He didn't care.'

Mandy had had her struggles with Adam over the years, she explained, because he was a free spirit. He didn't like school and preferred not to go. He lived for his horse – a stocky black and white creature, similar to the horses you often see on traveller sites. In fact, Adam thought of himself as a traveller.

'I used to dream of being a traveller,' Adam told me. 'I was a traveller in a past life – and I was hoping to be one again when I grew up. They used to call me 'Gadget,' you know.'

'Yes, we did!' said Mandy. 'That was his nickname. He was always making things. He made himself a trailer to go on the back of his bike and he used to cycle round the estate, collecting people's tat and then selling it. Some weeks, he made more money than I did at my job!'

'As long as I could make enough to feed my horse, I was happy,' Adam went on. 'I cleaned windows too. 50p a time, I charged, but it adds up. I just used to knock on doors around the estate, and when the ladies answered I'd say, 'D'you want your windows cleaned, love? Only 50p.' Most took me up on it.'

He was obviously quite an entrepreneur, young Adam. He could have gone far. How sad his life had been cut short, so tragically.

'I think, to get an idea who was responsible, it would be helpful to see where the accident took place,' I said to Mandy, as Adam moved away.

'That's no problem,' said Mandy. 'It's a big main road not far from us.'

As it happened, Dean knew the area she mentioned, so a few days later he drove me up there. It was the first time he'd seen me work so he was quite intrigued to watch what happened.

Walsall Road turned out to be a wide, straight highway, partially lined with tall trees, but very busy. Close to the M6 motorway, it was partly dual carriageway, and I expect the traffic that roared by was often moving pretty fast.

Poor Mandy was close to tears as she pointed out the spot

where they found Adam. There was nothing to see now, of course. It was just another stretch of tarmac, but as I stared at it, Adam suddenly joined us.

The others couldn't see him, but I watched as Adam stalked about the roadside in his trademark shorts and wellies, waving his arms about, as he tried to show me the direction the car had been travelling, the direction he himself had come from and the point where they'd collided. He was obviously still angry about the whole incident.

'I was just crossing the road on my bike,' said Adam, 'and then this car appeared. He was a horrible person, that driver. A really horrible person. He was driving way too fast, and he was looking at his mobile when he knocked me down.

'I hit his windscreen, my head smashed right into it. I saw his face and he saw mine – I know he did. But you know what he did then, Diane? He got out of the car and ran away. He left me to die. He just left me to die in the road. Didn't even call an ambulance.'

Adam even told me the name of the driver.

'I know who you're talking about,' Mandy said when I passed this information on.

Unfortunately, though the police investigated, there wasn't enough evidence, it turned out, to convict the culprit Adam had named.

Mandy was desperately disappointed, but Adam just shrugged when the news came through.

'He won't get away with it Diane,' he promised. 'I'm going to haunt him. I am. I'll haunt him. He'll be sorry!'

I had to smile to myself. I bet he would too. That cowardly driver doesn't know what he's let himself in for!

Adam was a real ray of sunshine when we chatted and he was obviously happy enough in the spirit world with his grandparents and several beloved dogs. However, there was no disguising the fact, the accident was a dreadful tragedy for his family. As a mum with a son not that much older than Adam, I could really feel for Mandy.

Dean was moved by her plight too. It was such a sad, sad case.

As we drove away we both felt we'd like to do some small thing to ease Mandy's pain. Adam could never be replaced, of course, but in the end we had a bench made for the family garden, with a plaque in memory of Adam, decorated with a picture of a horse, just like his beloved pet.

Now, Mandy tells me, she loves to sit out there to think about her boy, and she swears, when she does, she feels him close. Her instincts are completely correct. Half the time when Mandy's out there on the bench, Adam is sitting right beside her.

Fifteen

It was late on a mild, spring night. Warm light was spilling from an inviting looking pub beside a country road. The faint sounds of Irish music drifted jauntily across the carpark, along with raucous singing, stamping feet and waves of laughter that threaded uproariously through the melody. A good time was clearly being enjoyed by all inside.

Out here in the quiet dark, a sliver of crescent moon played hide and seek with the clouds, while the breeze rolling down from the mountains ruffled the grass at my feet and picked up the scent of lilacs from some unseen garden in the village.

It could have been an idyllic evening, but I knew it wasn't. In fact, I didn't like it one bit. There was a grim, sick feeling in my stomach. Despite the jollity nearby, something horrible was about to happen, I knew it.

The next second, a group of men burst through the shadows, dragging another individual between them. Their captive clearly had no wish to go with them. He was struggling and bucking, trying to pull out of their grip, but one of the men punched him viciously to his knees, another grabbed his hair and they threw him into the back of a waiting car.

The next thing I knew, the vehicle was speeding away, heading towards the border.

'Yes, I can see how they took him,' I said out loud, as the scene faded and I was standing outside the same pub, Three Steps, in bright daylight, forty years on.

Documentary maker, Alan Barry, was standing beside me. Alan had got in touch a few days before. He'd seen me on the internet, he explained, and he wondered if I might be able to go to Northern Ireland for the weekend to help with his film.

He was investigating the fate of British soldier Robert Nairac, who had been working undercover in Ireland during the 'troubles' of the 1970s.

Apparently, Robert had left his barracks, one evening in May 1977, to meet an important contact, at the Three Steps pub, near the border. He never returned. In fact, he was never seen again. It was quite clear he was dead, but even after all this time, the IRA had never revealed where his body was hidden.

Robert's disappearance troubled Alan Barry greatly.

'I was still at school when Robert Nairac was murdered,' Alan said, 'but later, I served in the same regiment – the Grenadier Guards.'

I'm sure the whereabouts of one of their fellow officers, a missing hero who'd gone on to be awarded the George Cross, posthumously, must have been a frequent topic of conversation in the regiment's mess. So much so, that when Alan eventually left the service, with still no answer to the mystery of where Captain Nairac was buried, he was inspired to make it his quest to find the remains of the murdered soldier, and finally bring him home.

'Sometimes in this life you have to stick your head above the parapet,' said Alan ruefully. 'I've always been one to see things through to the end. And should you find where he's buried Diane, if I have to go back there with a JCB and 20 Grenadier Guards, I'll do it. I just feel I have to send him home. His elderly sisters deserve to bury their brother.'

Alan turned out to be a real English gentleman, when we met at the airport. Still strongly built, with the straight backed, confident walk of the former soldier, he wasn't particularly tall, but with his distinguished head of thick grey hair and beautifully cultured British accent, he caught your attention immediately. He was so sincere about finding his missing comrade, I didn't have the heart to refuse.

Besides, though I hadn't heard of the case before, I was

intrigued to know what could have happened to this brave young man.

First stop in the beautiful green, green hills of Northern Ireland, not far from the border, was The Three Steps pub – the last place Robert Nairac was seen alive.

We pulled up outside in the little car Alan had borrowed from his son, who now lived in Ireland. If I'd been expecting a sinister, forbidding den, I'd have been very disappointed.

Set back from the road, The Three Steps turned out to be a long, low, white-painted building, with its name inscribed proudly across the gable in voluptuous, folksy script. Now declaring itself to be the Three Steps Bar and Lounge, I noticed. There was a large, airy car park, flower-speckled grassy verges, and perched on a small rise more or less next door, a handsome church looked down on the revellers. These days Three Steps welcomed families, walkers and tourists visiting the nearby beauty spots. You'd never have guessed that years ago this friendly place could have been the scene of violence and betrayal.

Unfortunately, the pub was closed that day but the owner kindly let us have a peek inside. We found ourselves looking at a large but cosy room with a gleaming bar down one side, polished floor and bright posters on the walls. As cheerful a place for a meal and a glass of your favourite bevvy as you could imagine.

As I stood there taking it all in, a vision of that night long ago flew into my mind. It was dark outside now and the place was Saturday-night rammed. There was a live band playing up one end, queues several deep at the bar, groups of friends jostling for space in the middle, and every table taken. And there in the thick of it, was Robert Nairac – a fit looking lad with dark hair, checked shirt, jeans and donkey jacket. Just like virtually every other young man in the place. He sounded like them too. Even though I knew he was English, I could hear Robert chatting away with such an effortless Irish twang, you'd have thought he was Belfast born and bred.

'I always mixed with the locals,' Robert said in my ear. 'It was my job, but I genuinely enjoyed being with them.'

His love for Irish music was genuine too. I could see him tapping his foot and clapping each tune, really enjoying himself. He would also sing along quite loudly to the Irish rebel songs, completely uninhibited. He seemed to know all the words. On the face of it, he appeared no different to any of the other Irish lads that night. Which was the whole point of course. His cover seemed amazingly authentic. Yet someone knew. And someone betrayed him.

Robert mentioned a name to me of the person who'd lured him there that night and I passed the name to Alan.

But Robert was a complex young man. As we spoke, he suddenly dropped the Irish accent, and his true, unmistakably English voice came through. He was very well spoken – we'd have reckoned him quite posh back in Swansea – and well educated too. How amazing that he can speak Irish so well, I thought. He must have been quite an actor.

He struck me as a confident and strong-minded person, and he had a great affinity with animals too. He told me he used to have a bird – a kestrel called Kes. Apparently, there'd been a film of the same name some years before, and one of the falcons used in the movie was actually Robert's pet. More recently he'd had a dog, a Pyrenean mountain dog and he was very sad to have been forced to leave him behind.

The link began to fade then, and Alan and I went back to the car. Outside the building, the events of that night in May were still clinging to my mind.

So... Robert had been inside the pub, passing himself off as an IRA sympathiser, I thought, then later in the evening he'd come out here and been set on and shoved into a vehicle.

'Okay, we'll go to another location I've heard about,' said Alan, swinging back into the road, and off we went again through the leafy country lanes. But all the way I kept getting flashes of that other trip, the one Robert had been forced to make, a confusing kaleidoscope of frightening scenes: dark fields; occasional headlights flaring out of the night; pitiless faces, packed in the car; and a helpless figure being punched.

Alan eventually pulled up near a farm. We were across the border now in Southern Ireland – Eire – though to be honest, the landscape looked much the same to me. As I got out the car, I saw Robert standing by a gate. He pointed silently through the entrance and immediately I was back in time again.

It was dark and I was looking at a bleak, gravelled area. The men had dragged Robert out of the car and were beating him up again. They'd torn his clothes off, stripped him naked and seemed to be trying to make him confess.

At one point he broke free and tried to run away but they went after him and hauled him back. One of them handed him a spade.

'Start digging your grave,' said the man. 'You're going to be killed tonight.'

Merciless though they were, I got the feeling these men weren't proper IRA members. They seemed disorganised and a bit unsure of what to do with their victim. One of the younger men kept running up the road to a phone box and making calls. Those were the days before mobile phones and I got the impression this man was calling the boss to report their progress and ask for further instructions.

Back in the gravel area, poor Robert was now forced to his knees again.

'Go on, beg for your life!' shouted one of the tormentors.

But Robert wouldn't. He was petrified. I could feel his terrible fear, yet battered, bruised and covered in blood as he was, he wouldn't tell them anything and he refused to beg.

Eventually, clearly realising they weren't going to get any information out of him, they dragged him again to a wooded area and shot him. In a way it was a relief. Robert died instantly and I could only be glad his suffering was over. It had been awful to see.

'They kept moving my body,' said Robert as we walked away. 'They buried me three times. At least three. They had to move me from the farm. They were afraid the animals would dig me up.'

Alan confirmed this was something researchers he'd consulted now believed had happened. The murderers, fearing the Captain's body would be discovered, kept digging him up and reburying him in different locations.

'We think he might have ended up somewhere in this forest,' Alan went on, as our road now took us through a vast wooded area – Ravensdale Forest, Alan told me it was called. 'Let me know if you get drawn to any spot.'

We drove on for a while, and then my stomach started to contract again and a particular group of trees seemed to jump out at me.

'Here Alan, stop here!' I said. Alan braked immediately and I leapt out of the car.

This is just like the Psychic Challenge TV task all over again, I thought to myself, as I slammed the car door behind me. Back then, I'd had to locate a man hidden in a wood – a real live man, camouflaged with leaves – and I'd walked straight through the undergrowth and found him, thankfully alive and well, with bracken in his hair!

This was very similar, except in this case, the hidden man was dead. Long dead. I stepped onto the springy, forest ground, all spongy under my feet. Some force was tugging at me like a magnet, drawing me forward into the trees. Movement caught my eye and I realised that, ahead of me, a shadowy group of men had become visible. They were staggering along, carrying an awkward bundle wrapped in some sort of thick material, possibly canvas. It was obviously heavy, and dipped in the middle like a sagging roll of carpet.

On they stumbled, complaining and swearing, while I hurried after them. Then, not far from the road, they suddenly stopped, dumped the bundle on the ground and began digging.

The vision dissolved and I walked forward and stepped on the place where I'd seen their spades break the soil.

'It was here,' I said to Alan. 'They buried him here.'

Alan was thrilled. He photographed the spot, measured the distance from the road and various trees, then we went off to explain it all to the police. I was exhausted by this time.

I find working so intensely in this way makes my blood sugar drop alarmingly, causing fatigue, but fortunately I found an old sweet lurking at the bottom of my coat pocket. It kept me going while we went over the details with the police. I was glad to find the police were not at all sarcastic. They'd heard of me before, they said, and were quite prepared to be open-minded. We went back to the forest, and they marked up the area properly, ready for further investigations.

After that, my work was done. I could only hope it was enough to help Alan get the answers he was looking for. As for me, I was looking forward to getting back to the hotel and having a rest. Dean and I had decided to stay on a little longer and have a mini-break in the beautiful area. It would be good to relax after such a harrowing case.

I left my number with Alan though, so he could keep me posted with any developments, and a few days later he phoned in great excitement. He'd gone back with specially trained cadaver dogs – the expert dogs that are used to sniff out dead bodies – he said, and in the place I'd indicated, they'd found the unmistakable scent of human remains.

This didn't prove they were the remains of Captain Nairac, of course, but it suggested that something more than dead leaves and soil lurked under that particular piece of ground.

The not so encouraging news, was that over the decades since Captain Nairac went missing, the forest and undergrowth had grown so dense with new trees and intertwining roots, it wasn't possible to dig the area by hand with spades, to unearth what the dogs had found.

Nevertheless, Alan was absolutely delighted. He hoped to go back soon to clear the area and excavate with mechanical diggers.

I was thrilled for him and so pleased he was pleased, though I had an uncomfortable feeling that nothing would come of it.

No matter how I concentrated, I couldn't see any further than what we'd found so far. It seems I was to be proved right.

As Alan tried to progress the case, he was met with incredulity that such an upheaval and expense should be requested on the word of a psychic. As far as I know, the site has not yet been excavated and poor Captain Nairac still remains in Ireland, where his murderers left him.

This is very sad for his poor family, obviously – but you know what? I suspect Robert himself is pretty settled in a better place these days, with his bird, and his dog, and the rest of his loved ones, and doesn't much care where those old remains might be.

Sixteen

Back at the hotel that night, it was good to be able to relax and let the distressing events of the day gradually fade away.

In fact, despite the horrors of the case, I was happy to be back in Ireland with Dean. It's such a beautiful country; it would be nice to explore it a little with my new man.

I've been lucky enough to visit Ireland many times over the years, sometimes to appear on TV or radio shows, but often to help out on baffling cases of disappearances or murders.

I'm sure the well-named Emerald Isle doesn't have more of these sad events than any other place, it's just that quite a few people in Ireland seem prepared to give us psychics the benefit of the doubt, and when conventional investigations draw a blank, they're quite happy to let us see if we can shed any light on unsolved mysteries.

'Yes, I've been here quite a few times,' I was saying to Dean, as we were sitting in the hotel restaurant looking through the menu. (Irish food is always delicious, so I was looking forward to a tasty dinner!)

Dean had brought me a glass of wine to help me unwind, and now, as we waited for our first course, I was sipping it gratefully and letting my memory float back over the Irish cases I'd worked on in the past.

Suddenly, a cheeky little face, framed with honey coloured hair tied in bunches, swam momentarily before my eyes, so vivid and bright I almost dropped my glass. Of course, I thought as the smiling child faded as quickly as she'd come. Mary.

'It's a little girl called Mary who sticks in my mind,' I said out loud to Dean. 'That case was near the border too, but on the republic side. Not round here where Captain Robert went missing – up on the opposite coast. It was so sad. She disappeared. She was only six. They call her Ireland's Madeleine McCann because, although there was a huge search, her body's never been found.'

'When did she go missing?' asked Dean.

I couldn't remember. It happened many years before I'd been called in, I knew that. Once again, it was a documentary maker who'd got me involved in the case. Just like Alan Barry, Steve was keen to solve a tantalising long-ago mysterious disappearance, and asked me to come and walk the scene with him, to see if I could pick up any clues.

'No, I really can't remember,' I repeated. 'Must have been decades ago.'

Intrigued, Dean started scrolling through his phone to look up the date.

'That's strange,' he said after a moment. 'Just look at this!'

He turned his phone round to show me the date he'd found. Little Mary Boyle had gone missing on March 18th 1977. Almost two months to the day before Captain Robert Nairac had vanished from the Three Steps pub in May, a hundred miles away. How very odd. Not that the two disappearances were in any way connected. But what a strange coincidence.

Steve, the documentary director, had first taken me to visit Mary's sister, Ann, because (perhaps even more tragically) the girls were identical twins and shared that special unique bond, so difficult for non-twins to understand.

Ann was a grown woman now, small and wiry, with shoulder-length brown hair. Looking at her, it was odd to think that by rights there should have been two Anns living near here – one woman the double of the other. Two attractive, capable ladies, who'd been here for each other, lives entwined, helping one another through their families' ups and downs. But, by some random stroke of fate, Mary and that shared future had been snatched away, and Ann was left to battle on alone, without her sister.

Even though so many decades had gone by, it was clear Ann still missed Mary desperately and believed her own life had been blighted by the tragedy.

'We were identical to look at, but our personalities were different,' said Ann. 'Mary was always the outgoing one. I was shy and hung back a bit but Mary spoke for me. We were like two halves of one person. Since she's gone, it's like part of me's been missing all this time too. Though, the funny thing is, at important moments in my life, I feel Mary comes close to me. Somehow, she's there.'

As Ann said that, Mary's little face flashed into my mind for the first time.

'I really do,' Mary told me, 'I'm always watching over her. I send her little signs.' And it seemed Ann understood them, which was a blessing.

Despite being so young when her sister disappeared, Ann's memories of Mary had never faded and she never stopped wanting to find out what happened that dreadful day.

Even as I was talking to Ann, I was aware my Grandfather had moved in beside me and was sadly shaking his head. As I mentioned before, these days, different spirits tend to come along to help me with different types of cases; I'd learned by now that, though my Grandfather was never far away, he always drew in particularly close to help when I was dealing with a case involving a child who's been sexually abused. So although I didn't know the details yet, I understood straight away what we were dealing with here.

I tried to suppress a shudder. 'It would help if I could visit the place where Mary was last seen,' I said quickly, to Steve.

'No problem,' said Steve. 'It won't take long.' And we walked back to his car.

Apparently, that fateful week in 1977 the family had gone to visit Ann's grandparents, on their remote dairy farm near the ancient town of Ballyshannon. They were looking forward to a traditional family get-together, to celebrate Ireland's most famous holiday – St Patrick's day, on March 17th. No doubt the festivities went on late into the night, and the next afternoon, they settled down to a lazy family lunch in the farmhouse. Afterwards the children went out to play in the garden. All that is, except Mary.

'Mary didn't come out with us straight away,' Ann recalled. 'She said she was going to help Mam with the dishes. That was typical Mary. I wasn't so interested in washing up, as she was. So I left her to it and went out to play with our older brother and two cousins. I expected Mary to be along after she'd done the dishes. It never occurred to me that she wouldn't come.'

But sadly, Mary didn't arrive and Ann never saw her again. Not a single trace of the child, not so much as a hair ribbon, has ever been found from that day to this. It was as if the ground had opened up and swallowed her whole.

A baffling story indeed, I thought as we bounced along the uneven country roads. The journey to the old family farmhouse took us through the most exquisite landscape of hills and lakes and bogs. The view was so peaceful and unspoiled, you'd have thought this area was the ideal place for children. Here they could run free, surely? Hard to imagine any serious harm could come to a small girl in this quiet place – unless she'd fallen into one of those bogs, of course.

Still, I had a bad feeling. The arrival of my Grandfather to help with the communication only confirmed my forebodings.

Eventually, we came off the rural road and bumped to the end of an overgrown track. There, shaded by straggly conifers, which may not have even been there in Mary's day, we came to a dilapidated building. Long and low, with a wide porch, country views and stained walls that may once have been white, back in 1977 the farmhouse must have been a pleasant home. But now it was as if the building had lost all hope, after Mary vanished. It had a haunted, abandoned air.

I stared at the scruffy patch of gloomy grass that was all that remained of the garden where Ann and her cousins had played. Then, as I turned back towards the house, I caught a glimpse of a small figure in a lavender top, brown trousers and black wellingtons, trotting past.

'I wanted to go with Uncle Gerry,' said Mary, tossing her long honey hair, bright ribbons bobbing.

I blinked and she was gone.

Ann explained that, though none of the children had seen Mary leave, they found out afterwards that instead of coming to play when the dishes were done, Mary had spotted her Uncle Gerry walking across the fields to return a ladder to a neighbour's farm, and for some reason, she'd run after him.

Gerry confirmed this later when he got back from delivering the ladder and stopping for a chat with the neighbour. Mary had followed him part of the way, he said, but then got fed up and turned back when they'd come to a bog which would have been tricky for her to cross. He last saw her heading for home, and was surprised to find she hadn't got back to the farmhouse before he did.

The bog Mary stopped at was thoroughly checked in the search that followed, just in case she'd changed her mind, tried to follow her uncle again, and fallen in while attempting to cross, but the bog was empty. Whatever happened to Mary, she'd not drowned there.

The whole episode was a puzzle.

I stared at the mournful scene again, willing it to give up its secrets.

'Come on Mary,' I coaxed silently, pacing up and down the faded grass. 'I saw you just now. Show me what happened.'

And then suddenly I felt myself tugged forwards and it was almost as if I'd landed inside Mary's body, seeing what she saw — or rather, finding myself unable to see, but sensing instead. I felt strong hands grab me, then something thick and dusty was pulled down rapidly over my head and I was snatched up, almost choking from the rough, grimy material pressed tight against my mouth, and carried briskly away.

The next thing I knew, I was tossed, sprawling onto a hard concrete floor and big, tough hands were tearing at my trousers. I was struggling and kicking out with my black wellies but it was no good. The man was far too strong and powerful.

The scene was so distressing, I had to pull back and put some distance between me and poor little Mary. She was raped, I know that, then strangled — presumably so there was no way she could ever tell anyone what had been done to her.

It was like being forced to watch a horror film. I could only stare helplessly as her tiny, lifeless body was stuffed into a sack, before, mercifully, the scene faded.

The next second, the film was running again. We were in a different location now. It was later in the day, or maybe even a different day. The light was draining out of the sky, it was almost dark and in front, I could see a silvery lake glimmering amongst fields and wildflowers. A lovely place for a picnic on a summer's afternoon, you might think. Except that now I looked closer, I could see the grass was so densely packed around the water's edge and so high, there was nowhere to spread out a rug.

As I watched, a man wearing tall waders came forcing a path through the chest high vegetation, a bulging sack over his shoulder. In the distance, over the top of the grasses, I could just make out a battered old vehicle pulled up at the side of the track behind him. I turned back. The man was still carving a slow, snaking trail through the undergrowth. It was hard going, but he was clearly determined to reach the lake.

Eventually he came to the water's edge, but when he broke through the tight fringe of grass and reeds, the bank was so steep, he slithered and fell, rather than climbed, down into the water. Unfazed, he found his feet, steadied the sack and bent to pick something up from the bottom. It was a large rock. He dropped it in the sack, stooped again to collect another two and dropped them in for good measure. Then he tied the top of the sack and paddled out into the water, dragging it after him.

Out and out he went, until the water was up to his chest, then he pulled the sack round in front of him, and with both hands, pushed it firmly down below the surface. It sank immediately. He stood there for a while, waiting to see if it would float back up. It didn't. Satisfied, he turned and made his way back to the shore.

As the scene dissolved, I heard the culprit's name – which I passed on to Steve and Ann.

Steve, who'd been recording the whole thing, quickly dug out some large Ordnance Survey-type maps from the car.

'D'you think you can pinpoint that lake Diane?' he asked.

I was still feeling a bit drained and numb from the unpleasant experience but I tore myself away from Mary, and went over to look at the paper sheets he'd unfolded and spread out in front of me. I was surprised to see there was quite a lot of water marked in the area, including several lakes. There was even a lake very close to the family farmhouse. Half closing my eyes, I squinted at the sheet, trying to see without seeing. Would any of these places speak to me? After a few seconds my finger started to tingle and it felt as if it was being dragged across the map until it came to rest on one particular patch of blue.

'That's the lake,' I said to Steve. 'She's in there.'

Steve peered to see which lake I was pointing at, then he stepped back in amazement. He knew that lake, it seemed.

'Oh my God! That would be the ideal place to put somebody,' he said. 'It's so awkward to get to, nobody goes there – ever. They don't even fish there because it's so difficult. If you wanted to dispose of a body it would be perfect.'

As Steve was speaking, my Grandfather suddenly appeared next to him. Grandfather was nodding approvingly. I'd obviously understood what he'd been trying to tell me. He'd been by my side, guiding me through the whole difficult experience. He loathed child abuse cases as much as I did but he believed we owed it to the families to help them discover the truth.

Now though, it was time for us to withdraw.

Just as in the Captain Nairac case, I realised my work for this visit was done. There was nothing more I could do. It was down to Steve now. He planned to take all our information to the police, then he hoped to return with frogmen to search the lake as soon as the necessary permissions could be organised. I do hope, for the sake of the whole family, they find Mary so that after all these years, they can finally lay her to rest.

It's a strange thing, but as well as helping me uncover child abuse cases, it's almost as if my Grandfather's passed on to me a kind of radar to detect paedophiles. These days, the minute I see someone with an unsavoury secret, a deep green aura appears around their whole body. It's like an inner poison radiating out.

I suppose the knack was already beginning to develop when I was a child. One day, coming home from school, I was sitting on the bus wondering what we might be having for tea that night, when I became aware of a man in a seat nearby. He was a perfectly ordinary looking man, and I wouldn't say he was staring at me exactly, yet there was something about him that made me nervous. As soon as I saw him, I just knew he was going to get off at the same stop as I did, and follow me.

The closer we came to my stop, the more my stomach tied

itself in painful knots. My hands began to feel clammy, my mouth dry, and by the time the bus jerked to a standstill at my stop, I had half a mind to stay where I was. I was safe on the bus. Trouble was, I had to get off some time and it would be even worse if I leapt off in a strange street I didn't know and got lost, with that man behind me.

Desperately, just before the bus moved again, I leapt to my feet and hopped off. I'd left it till the last possible minute, but out of the corner of my eye I could see the man had jumped off too.

I started up the road as briskly as I could but I could feel him behind me and getting closer. Abruptly, I crossed the road and increased my pace, but then he did too. Beginning to panic, I recrossed the road several times but each time, he did the same, and the distance between us was getting smaller and smaller. There was no one around, not even a passing car and soon I would have to turn the corner into an even quieter street.

'Go and knock on a door,' my Grandfather's voice said, suddenly in my ear.

'That one, just up there.'

I looked towards the house he was indicating. It was neat and tidy, with old-fashioned net curtains in the windows and a tiny scrap of garden at the front.

I had no idea who lived there. It could have been out of the frying pan into the fire. There might have been no one in, but I didn't hesitate. Positioning myself as if I was going to go straight on, I trotted almost past the house, then at the last second I turned sharply, swerved onto the front path and ran to hammer on the door.

To my relief it was opened almost immediately by an elderly woman.

'I'm so sorry to bother you,' I babbled, 'but there's a man following me and I'm scared.'

The woman took in my frightened face and school uniform, then she glanced over my head and saw the man skulking along a little further down the road, trying to look nonchalant.

'Don't you worry, pet,' she said. 'Come in for a minute. My husband will walk you home.'

The next thing I knew her grey haired husband appeared in the hall.

'Just let me change out of me slippers, pet,' he said, 'and I'll be with you.'

A few minutes later he was back in outdoor shoes, a warm coat and carrying a stout umbrella.

'In case he tries anything!' he said, jokily brandishing the umbrella like a club and giving me a wink.

By the time we were back in the street, the man had gone, but the kindly old gentleman escorted me right to my front door all the same, and waited until he'd seen me safely inside, before turning and heading home.

Thank goodness my Grandfather had told me what to do or I dread to think what might have happened.

From then on my sixth sense about paedophiles seemed to get stronger and stronger and the uncomfortable physical sensations that swept over me when I encountered a person with unhealthy interests, began to be accompanied by the ability to see the culprit's aura as well.

Not all auras denote bad character, of course. Most are quite the opposite. I'll never forget the time I noticed a tramp sitting in Castle Square, Swansea. He was wearing a distinctive woolly hat and I discovered later he was well known in the area as 'Teacosy Pete,' on account of his unusual headgear.

More distinctive to me though, as I caught sight of him that day, was the brilliantly bright aura that shone around him, as if he was seated in front of the sun.

You could just tell he was intelligent and caring – a really kind man. He never begged and he wasn't on drugs or alcohol and when you spoke to him it was obvious he was well-educated. It made you wonder how he could have ended up on the streets.

'He's very sensitive,' my Grandfather murmured in my ear, 'A gifted man but some people just can't cope with their intelligence and tender feelings. The world is too much for them.'

I gave Pete money whenever I passed, and I knew I'd be helping other people too because Pete was a man who shared. He never smoked, but he'd spend half the day picking up cigarette ends to give to the other tramps who did. Apparently, once, he found a wallet on the ground containing £300 and walked 12 miles to the owner's house to return it, refusing any sort of reward.

I was very sad to read, years later in 2015, that he'd died suddenly. That's when it emerged he'd been a school friend of former Archbishop of Canterbury, Dr Rowan Williams, but had renounced the rat-race and taken to the streets at an early age, after the double blows of being rejected by Oxford University and losing his beloved brother in a tragic accident.

Though maybe his special gifts weren't wasted after all. At his funeral, hundreds of people lined the streets and stood outside the church to pay their respects. It was clear that despite his modest means and unassuming manner, he'd touched a great many hearts.

The same will never be said about that creepy man in the tea shop who tried to lend me his books, I'm quite sure. His hideous green aura marked him out as the type of man people would instinctively back away from, even if they couldn't see what he was radiating.

I came across the same sort of phenomenon a couple of years later when I decided to take a walk along the shore at the Mumbles. It was midsummer, a really beautiful day, and I never need an excuse to be beside the seaside. Despite the troubles at home during my childhood, the pier at the Mumbles was the scene of some of my happiest memories. My brothers, sister and I would escape down to the seafront clutching our paper bags of homemade sandwiches. We'd race onto the pier, where we stuffed any coins we'd managed to scrounge, into the slot machines, then we'd chase up and down the deck, and go fishing off the end.

Gary fixed me up with a little fishing rod and dug for lug worms on the beach to use as bait, then we'd stand there for hours watching our lines bobbing on the waves. We seldom caught anything but we always had fun.

So now, this particular day, with an hour to spare before I needed to be anywhere, I drove back to my happy place, intending to enjoy a quiet stroll. As I pulled into the car park, I noticed a motorbike cruising in behind me. I was reaching for my sunglasses and my bag, but something made me pause and watch the bike in my mirror. It rolled to a stop quite close to my car, and the rider climbed heavily off.

Instantly, my stomach began to clench. I glanced over at the man. He was wearing one of those full-face helmets, all black and opaque, that always look a bit sinister to me. But just then, he lifted it off, and if anything, I felt even worse.

He was thick-set with greasy hair, flattened from the helmet and a flabby paunch straining at his leather jacket. Just the sight of him made me feel as sick as I did when the creepy customer appeared in the tea-room, and as I stared, the telltale poison green aura appeared all round his body.

For the moment, he seemed quite unaware of my gaze. Something else had caught his attention down on the shore. I turned to see what he was looking at. There, at the water's edge, a group of boys and girls aged around 10 were playing. The boys were bare chested, dressed only in shorts, and the girls wore skimpy summer tee-shirts knotted up at the hem so they could tan their tummies. They were larking around, as kids do, giggling, splashing each other and jumping in, completely unaware of the man who was watching them like a cat stalking a bird.

I know what you're here for, I thought to myself.

'You're right Diane,' Grandfather said suddenly in my head. 'Don't doubt that feeling you have.'

As Grandfather spoke, the motorcyclist started to walk towards the children. Quickly, I flew out of the car and dashed after him. Once I drew level, I began to walk the same way, at the same pace, but a few metres apart. I'd intended to head for the pier that afternoon but now that was impossible. I couldn't leave the children.

Closer and closer the motorcyclist strolled. I wanted to shout out to the kids, 'Don't speak to that man! Don't trust him!' but of course I couldn't. He hadn't actually done anything yet.

So instead, I made quite sure he could see me. I sat myself down on a bench and stared and stared at him, beaming hostility in his direction – killing him with my eyes. If he dared to go right up to the children and start talking to them, I'd have to jump up and intervene. Heaven knows what I'd say but I'd think of something.

Fortunately, it wasn't necessary. As I watched, the man became more and more uncomfortable. He kept darting nervous little glances in my direction to see if I was still staring, then quickly looking away when he saw I was. His feet were moving slower and slower and his confident swagger had wilted.

'Does she know me?' he was thinking – I could almost see the words running through his head. 'Will she tell anyone?'

His feet stopped altogether and he came to a standstill a few metres from the children. He glanced, with uncertainty, from the kids, to me, and back again. There was a long pause. Then, with an annoyed little jerk, he turned and walked quickly back to his motorbike. Scowling in my direction, he pulled the helmet back over his head, climbed onto the bike and roared angrily away.

'Well done,' said Grandfather's voice in my head. 'You're listening. There are some evil people in the world.'

'Thanks Grandfather,' I replied silently.

And there I sat for a while longer. I had to make sure he wouldn't come back. So I watched the children innocently playing until I was quite sure the man was gone for good and they were safe. Then I rose and headed for the pier, to continue my walk down memory lane.

Seventeen

OMG! I looked down at the palm of my hand in horror. There, cradled in the centre, was a little creamy white scrap of what looked like plastic – only it wasn't plastic, well not as far as I know anyway, it was the crown of one of my side teeth, which, only a few moments before as I put on my lipstick in the mirror, had been sitting happily in the corner of my smile.

Disaster! Dean and I were literally just about to leave for a short break in Bath, to meet the actress Kym Marsh and watch her in her new play, Fatal Attraction. I was so excited to meet Kym in person, after years as online Twitter friends, and naturally I wanted to look my best. Now I'd turn up looking as if I'd been in a fight!

The car was all packed and we were ready to go but: 'Dean!' I shouted, 'I've got to get to the dentist!'

'Sorry – what did you say?' a baffled Dean called back.

'Emergency dentist! Disaster!' I cried, hurrying out of the bathroom, the crown in my hand. I was starting to lisp already, I was sure of it. Every time I tried to speak, my tongue went straight to the big gap where my tooth should be. I could have wept.

Dean, bless him, was marvellous. He phoned my dentist, then several others but none of them could see me at such short notice. The earliest appointment was the following week.

I was in despair. I didn't want to miss the play, or my meeting with Kym, but there was no way I was going to turn up with a dark hole in my face where my tooth should be. And I could hardly keep my lips clamped tightly shut throughout – Kym would think it strange if I didn't speak!

'I know,' said Dean. 'Gorilla Glue! Supposed to stick anything.

We'll stick it back on ourselves.'

I had my doubts, but it was worth a try. After all, didn't the dentist do something similar? So off Dean went to his van and returned a few minutes later with the glue. I lay in a chair, tilting my head back as far as it would go, while Dean did his best to wrestle that pesky little crown back over my tooth. This is not how I imagined our romantic break in Bath would begin, I remember thinking to myself, as Dean loomed over me.

Well he struggled valiantly, but it was no use. After every effort the ungrateful crown fell straight back out again.

Still, this was no time to give up. I sat up quickly.

'I'll see if I can do it,' I said, 'My fingers are smaller. It might be easier for me.' I decided to adopt the scientific approach too.

Fetching my hairdryer I opened my mouth wide and carefully played the hot air over my gums and front teeth to get the area as dry as possible. Then with a tooth-pick, I dabbed a tiny bead of glue into the crown and also onto the stub of my tooth. I waited a moment or two to let the glue start to go off, then I jammed the crown back in place. To my amazement it held. I was a bit nervous about biting anything or even clamping my jaw together too firmly at first, but after a while the tooth remained strong, so strong in fact, I was able to forget about it.

Well what d'you know? I thought as we finally set off for Bath, only an hour or two behind schedule, Gorilla Glue really does seem to stick just about anything!

Thank goodness I'd be able to meet Kym without embarrassment. Even so, I refused to eat anything, in any way solid, throughout the visit, just in case.

Kym wasn't the first celebrity I've met over the years of course. I've been lucky in that my work has brought me into contact with quite a few famous faces along the way.

Oddly enough though, the first one was nothing to do with my gift. Years ago Mum asked me to go along to bingo with her. We often went together but this was to be a very exciting night she promised, as the famous astrologer, Russell Grant, was coming to give out the big prize.

We dolled ourselves up the way we always enjoyed doing for our bingo nights. I had a lovely white dress with black splashes all over it, I seem to remember, and of course being me, my hair and makeup had to be perfect. Then, satisfied we looked our best, off we went to the converted church hall which now served as our bingo palace.

The whole place was already buzzing when we arrived. Whether it was the big prize on offer, or the appearance of a celebrity, I wasn't sure, but whatever the reason, the atmosphere was thrilling. What's more, one of my old school friends was there with her mum too, and they took seats in the row just in front of us so we could chat backwards and forwards over the chair backs. My friend had no money that day, she told me, but she was so determined not to miss Russell Grant, she'd borrowed the cash from her mum.

The audience buzz grew louder and louder as the minutes passed, and then suddenly the lights blazed, and the ebullient figure of Russell Grant bounced onto the stage, black curls tossing and gleaming in the glare. He looked exactly the way he looked on TV.

After a brief introduction, he paused dramatically and gazed out at us in the audience, theatrically scanning his eyes up and down the rows of seats as if he was could tell exactly who he was looking for.

'*Somebody* in this place tonight,' he intoned knowingly, 'is going to win the big money!' and slowly he lifted his arm, swung it teasingly along the rows, until it stopped and he was pointing ...straight at... me!

I could hardly breathe. Was it me? Did he mean me? Or could it be the row in front, or maybe the row behind?

'And by the way love,' Russell went on cheekily, 'you're a Libra!'

I gasped. He did mean me. I *am* a Libra! I was so impressed he did that.

Sadly, as it turned out he wasn't to be quite so spot on with picking the winner. I didn't win a thing that night, but amazingly, my friend sitting just in front did. She won the big prize of £25,000 – a fabulous sum nowadays of course, but back then a small fortune! And she received her cheque, personally, from Russell Grant's own hands. She was beyond ecstatic.

Disappointing for me, though I was pleased for my friend, but considering how many people were in the hall, it was a pretty impressive piece of psychic work for Russell to have got so close to finding the winner. It was clear this man wasn't just an astrologer. He was psychic as well.

But that memorable night wasn't to be the end of my encounter with Russell. I followed his career fondly from then on, and so I was delighted when a few years later, after winning Britain's Psychic Challenge I got a call from the producer of the Russell Grant show, asking if I'd like to appear. They would pay for my train ticket to London, said the producer. Then I'd just have to do a small psychic reading. Fine by me, I thought.

It was another exciting day. I hadn't actually spent any time with Russell Grant back at the bingo hall of course, but now I discovered he was kind, entertaining and a genuinely funny guy. He was dressed in a quirky looking shiny purple suit – fun for the cameras – and came forward to greet me and the other psychic lady who'd been invited on the show, with a friendly smile. He quickly put us at ease, then he handed me a ring.

'What can you tell us about this ring?' he asked.

I found myself looking down at a huge lump of gold, studded

with rubies, the bright stones embedded deep into the metal. It was a big, chunky piece of jewellery weighing heavy in my hand, and as I held it I could feel the love radiating out into my skin.

'This belongs to you Russell,' I said, 'and it means a lot to you. It was given to you by your partner. You love this ring.'

Russell agreed that he did.

On another occasion, I was invited back on the show and once again Russell came to greet me in his trademark eye-dazzling outfit.

'We've got some young lads for you to read for today,' he confided, as he led me into the studio.

The next thing I knew, four cheerful, energetic young men, not much older than my Lisa, were crowding round wanting to know if they were going to be famous. They called themselves McFly they said, after the young hero of the film Back to the Future, one of their favourite movies.

'Yes!' I was able to tell them. 'You're going to be household names, with many hit records to come.'

Which not only pleased them very much, but it's also exactly what happened.

Once social media got up and running a few years later, it became easier for us all to get in touch with people whose work interested us. I was amazed and delighted to find a number of well-known people were becoming my internet friends, including Bonnie Tyler, my incredibly talented near neighbour in Swansea; comedian, Keith Lemon; TV presenter, Eamonn Holmes; and of course, Kym Marsh.

With Kym it happened by accident. I don't normally get the chance to watch the soaps, but one evening I happened to be home and not in the kitchen cooking, when Coronation Street came on, so I settled down to watch it for a change. Straight away, my eyes were drawn to a young actress who'd recently joined the cast. But she wasn't foremost an actress, I'd heard, this Kym Marsh had recently been a singer in the famous band Hear'Say. A good singer by all accounts.

Yet here she was acting in a prime-time TV soap and making an amazingly professional job of it. How talented did you have to be to achieve success in both fields, I wondered in awe as I watched her. I could see this young woman would go far.

So not long after that, out of pure curiosity, I started following her on Twitter, just to see what she'd do next. To my surprise, one of the things she did next was follow me right back!

And that's how it began. Occasionally I'd get little messages for Kym, often concerning her career, that I passed on to her and we began chatting quite frequently. Then last year, in October, bizarrely I had a dream about her. I knew straight away it wasn't an ordinary dream, it was one of my psychic wall scenarios playing itself out in my sleep.

'Kym,' I told her the next morning, 'I dreamed about you last night. You had fresh flowers in your hair and I saw your name in a wedding book.'

I think it's fair to say Kym was gobsmacked. 'Oh my heavens!' she said, 'I've told nobody, nobody. I wanted to keep it really quiet, but I'm getting married tomorrow and I'll be wearing fresh flowers in my hair.'

She and her fiancé had brought the wedding forward because Kym's father was seriously ill and they wanted to make sure he could attend.

'And you've been worrying because the weather's been bad this week,' I added, 'and you think it might spoil the day. Well stop worrying. The weather's going to be lovely and you'll have a wonderful day.'

She did too.

And so finally we got to meet a few months later in the gorgeous town of Bath. What's more, we discovered we were both staying in the same hotel, so the day after the show — which was brilliant, naturally — we slipped down to a quiet corner of the lounge for a chat.

Kym turned out to be as down to earth and fun as she seemed on screen, and she roared with laughter when I told her the sorry tale of my tooth. It certainly broke the ice!

'You'd never know!' she said, peering at my handiwork.

While we talked, a few more messages came through for her, including one from her late son — the poor little baby who'd been born premature at 21 weeks and passed away soon after, back in 2009.

'He's a tall, handsome young man now,' I told her, 'with beautiful blonde curls. He's with you always and he was by your side at the wedding.'

I paused. The boy's name was Archie. 'He keeps telling me to call him Jay?' I said. 'He's going on about Jay.'

Kym's mouth dropped open. 'That's his middle name,' she said, 'and now I've given it to my daughter Polly, his younger sister. She wants to be known as Jay, she says, from now on, and we've agreed.'

There were more family details and interesting news about her career. Exciting times are earmarked for Kym in the future, that's for sure.

Finally, it was time for Kym to get ready for the next show and me to head back to Swansea. After the potentially disastrous start, our short break had turned into a really memorable interlude — for all the right reasons!

'And the tooth's still going strong,' I said to Dean as we breezed along the M4 on our way home.

He laughed. 'You can't beat Gorilla Glue!'

Afterwards, Kym kindly sent me an account of our meeting for my records:

I've followed Diane for a few years on Instagram and we briefly exchanged messages but I'd never managed to get myself a reading in. However, we just so happened to find ourselves staying in the same hotel so it totally felt like fate that we were meant to be there on that day.

I've got to say I've never been so blown away! Speechless for the first time in my life. Diane knew specific names ...she was telling me about my Polly, getting her personality and interests spot on. She suddenly asked, 'Who is Finn? He is very important to Polly'. Well Finn is my nephew and he and Polly are best friends, they have a huge bond and this is something she could never have known.

She told me about things in my past and those around me. Things I have not spoken about publicly, personal things. She told me things about my sister and her partner, things I didn't even know to be true until I went back and asked my sister about them.

To sum up, it was just really, really amazing. I felt so comforted by the things she told me about loved ones who had passed away and felt buoyed by the things she said about those around me and the future of my loved ones.

I feel so lucky to have been in the hotel that day. Thank you Diane, you truly are a marvellous woman and now one of my friends,

Kym.

Such a lovely note. I was very touched.

There was an amusing postscript to our meeting as well. A week or two later when I finally got my appointment with the dentist, he was a bit fazed when he came to tackle my crown.

'My God!' he said, as he struggled to remove it, 'I've come across plenty of crowns people have stuck back themselves but I've never, ever come across one stuck so firmly as this!'

So well done Gorilla Glue, and I swear I don't have shares in the company!

Eighteen

Ping! Another email bounced into my inbox. I get a lot of emails but there was something about that 'ping' that sounded urgent. I glanced up from my appointments diary – I was trying to find a space to squeeze another client into a pretty complicated week, and I wasn't having much luck. To my surprise, the email was from my old friend, Kenny Delcassian.

I pushed away the diary. I hadn't heard from Kenny for quite a while. This must be important. Poor Kenny was the survivor of an awful murder case that ended up causing the deaths of three people, one of them his own wife, so I always dropped everything for Kenny, if I could.

'There's been a development in the case,' Kenny wanted me to know, and he sounded excited. 'I've had journalists with me the last few days. Looks like they're closing in on the mastermind! A file has been sent to the Director of Public Prosecutions.'

That was wonderful news. After many agonising years, with the killer, or killers, appearing to have got away with it, first one, then two perpetrators had been jailed. However, the culprit behind the whole crime, the person who ordered the murder – nicknamed by the police: 'the mastermind' – had so far escaped. Perhaps now, at last, there would be justice for the victims.

I'd first met Kenny and his wife Anne, well over a decade ago, when Anne got in touch to ask if I could help shed any light on the unsolved murder of her sister, Irene White. Anne now lived in England with her husband Kenny but she and Irene had been brought up in Ireland, which is where Irene was living at the time of her death.

'We saw you on TV, walking a murder scene and picking up

details,' Anne told me when she phoned. 'And we wondered if you could do the same for us? Any information we can find, no matter how small, would be helpful. So far the police don't seem to be getting anywhere.'

Anne was desperate to find her sister's killer and she was quite determined that if the police couldn't solve the mystery, she'd turn detective and do it herself.

Fortunately, at that time, I was doing a lot of TV work in Ireland, so on my next visit, accompanied as ever by my intrepid mum, I arranged to meet up with Anne and Kenny in Dundalk, where Irene and their mother had lived.

Dundalk turned out to be a handsome town on the Castletown River in the place where it flowed out into the broad waters of Dundalk Bay. Even though I couldn't see any sign of the sea when we stepped out of the taxi, you could smell that fresh, salty tang in the air that tells you the waves aren't far away. A bit like Swansea really, I joked to Mum.

Anne and Kenny were standing on the pavement waiting for us, and Anne hurried over at once. She was a smartly dressed, strong looking woman with thick dark hair and a warm smile. But anyone underestimating this lady, I thought to myself, would be in for a shock. Beneath that friendly manner, you could tell determination ran through her like the letters through a stick of rock.

'We thought we'd show you Irene's house first,' said Anne. 'This is where it happened.' She steered us across the road to a striking detached house, with ornamental gate posts in the front and a tall gate of solid wood at the side.

What an unusual place, I thought. Not at all what I'd expected. Painted a warm cream, the property was a typical, Art Deco design, with a flat roof, multi-paned windows, and an odd, irregular shape. The windows were odd too. At one end of the house, the corner was formed not by masonry but by two windows butted up against each other, each giving a view of a different direction. Slightly strange and quite unlike anything else in the street.

As I stood there, reaching out in my mind to Irene, a dreadful chill seemed to rise up from my feet and sweep through my whole body. Despite the mildly glowing colour of the paintwork, the house somehow managed to exude a deep, unpleasant cold.

'Oh... suddenly I'm freezing,' I said to Anne. It was all I could do to stop my teeth from chattering.

She smiled. 'Well the house *is* called the Ice House!' she said.

We laughed, but the name didn't refer to the temperature of the place. Anne explained that the park which lay just behind Irene's former garden, was known as Ice House Hill Park – named for the 17th century Ice House that was all that remained of a stately home and grand estate that once occupied the land. Irene's home must have been named after the historical feature.

Nevertheless, historical feature or not, I was still cold! I pulled my coat more tightly around me and forced myself to concentrate again. Almost at once, the sound of the traffic died away and the face of a beautiful woman in her prime, floated into my mind.

She had the most exquisite, creamy-white complexion, smooth and finely grained as silk, and a cloud of deep auburn hair framed her face. A real beauty was Irene, that much was clear. She gave me a shy smile, as if to say 'hello,' then she seemed to gesture behind her. I looked in the direction she indicated and then recoiled in horror. I was staring at blood. Blood and then more blood. Blood everywhere. Blood all over the floor, all over Irene, that delicate complexion all stained and spattered with blood...

It was horrific. I pulled away from the terrifying scene, but then of course I had to look some more. Now I was seeing a confused impression of Irene, full length this time, and bizarrely, wearing orange rubber gloves. I could see a sink with washing up in it, and a man standing over Irene, stabbing and stabbing and stabbing.

'He came in the back,' said Irene in my ear. 'He said he'd come to tell me my gate was open...'

I tried to focus on the attacker. He was young, very young, and powerfully built, with hair so dark it was almost black. He seemed to be going crazy. He couldn't stop stabbing and slashing at poor Irene. He must have stabbed her at least thirty times.

But when at last he seemed to realise Irene was quite still (was never going to move again in fact) so there was no point in stabbing any more, it was as if he was appalled at what he'd done. The arm holding the knife dropped to his side and an anguished expression flitted over his face. He stood there for a moment staring down at Irene, and then to my amazement, he mouthed a prayer over her body.

The next second, he was out along the hall and running.

'He doesn't live in the town,' I said to Anne. 'He comes from somewhere outside. You won't find him in Dundalk.'

'There's a detective from the garda out in the car,' said Anne, when I'd finished. 'D'you think you can tell him what you told us?'

'Of course,' I said, so a few minutes later there I was, sitting in the car, describing my gruesome impressions to the policeman.

'He ran away over a sort of bank beside the house,' I explained, as I finished. 'He didn't come back out into the street so I don't suppose anyone passing in the road would have seen him leave. He was covered in blood.'

'How do you know these things?' asked the policeman, totally perplexed.

I gathered from that, that various details I'd described, particularly the extreme viciousness of the attack and the direction in which the killer had fled, were correct, yet not yet widely known.

'And I'll tell you something else,' I added. 'It's no use looking for him round here. Or even in Ireland. He's gone abroad.'

'Okay, we just want to take you to another address now if that's alright,' said Anne, when the detective had finally written down everything I'd told him and set off back to the police station. 'See what you make of this.'

So Mum and I piled into the back of the Delcassians' car and Kenny drove us through the town centre and out into a quieter area that seemed to skirt the bay.

As he drove, Kenny filled us in a bit more on what had happened that awful day back in April 2005.

'Over in England, Anne and I had been rushing around all morning after a late night the night before,' said Kenny, 'so we went up to take a rest on our bed. Next thing we knew, a bird slammed into the bedroom window. It was really odd. Anne turned to me and said, 'That's a sign of a death that is. It's a bad omen.' Thirty minutes later, the phone rang and we got the news of the murder.'

Apparently the sisters' elderly mother, Maureen, lived in a mobile home at the bottom of the Ice House garden, where Irene could keep an eye on her, and she used to pop in every morning for a cup of tea and a chat with her daughter. That day, around noon, she'd wandered up the garden path as usual, to find the back door swinging open. Puzzled, she carried on into the kitchen and stumbled upon a scene of unimaginable horror. It would have been a terrible sight for a complete stranger to have to witness, but when it was your own loved one lying there in a pool of blood, the shock must have been indescribable. By all accounts, the poor woman never recovered. She died six months later, on what would have been Irene's 43rd birthday.

In the back of the car, I bit my lip. The whole story was just getting worse and worse. Mum and I exchanged appalled looks. Irene left behind three children, Anne went on. The youngest, only five years old. In fact, she'd only just got back from dropping the little ones at school when the killer struck.

'Ah, here we are,' said Kenny suddenly, and he pulled up outside a neat detached house, in what seemed to be a quiet suburb. The day had flown by and it was starting to get dark now. We all stared at the house, glimmering quietly in the twilight. I wasn't sure why we'd come here so I began to reach out to see what impressions I could pick up.

What could have happened in this pleasant looking place? I wondered.

Just then, over in the house, a light flicked on in a downstairs window and the silhouette of a man came into view. He passed back and forth, apparently beginning some chore. After a moment or two, he moved towards the window and we saw him lift a couple of plates and dip them down below the sill. Of course. This was the kitchen and he was washing up. The light gleamed on his bald head.

'Oh my God,' I said suddenly, as another revelation struck me. 'That man's part of it!'

'He didn't do the stabbing,' said Irene's voice in my head, 'but he's definitely involved.'

Anne swung round, a satisfied smile on her face. 'That's all I wanted to hear,' she said. 'We suspected him and you've just confirmed it. Thank you Diane.'

The man couldn't possibly have heard what we were saying but at that moment, as if some sixth sense alerted him, he seemed to notice our car for the first time. He was looking out from a lighted room, and we were sitting in the dark, so he couldn't have made us out in the blackness of the car's interior, but instantly a blind rattled down over the window and he disappeared.

'Oh well, we might as well be off then,' said Anne after a moment or two. 'But thank you, Diane. That proves it.'

It turned out this man, whose name was Niall Power, was known to Irene and her family. He'd fitted the security gates on her home. Not long before the murder, the gates seemed to develop a fault and Irene kept asking him to fix them, but somehow, he'd never got round to it.

At the time of her death, Irene who worked as a reflexologist, was living alone as a single mum in the big house after separating from her husband. They were getting a divorce and the house was to be sold, but until then, Irene was on her own in the place, with just the children for protection. No wonder she was nervous about the insecure gates.

When Anne and Kenny arrived in Ireland after hearing the tragic news, they were told by one of Irene's friends that Irene had even been getting death threats in the weeks leading up to the killing.

'It was the first we'd heard of it,' said Anne, 'but it's not surprising she was frightened.'

Then, later, at the funeral home, when they were making arrangements for Irene's funeral, Kenny bumped into Niall Power, who was standing in the car park with a couple of other men. Presumably, Niall was there to pay his hypocritical respects. Kenny took one look at Niall and saw guilt written all over his face.

'I just knew,' said Kenny, 'and he knew I knew, as well. He looked terrified.'

But knowing instinctively was one thing. Finding the evidence to convict was another matter entirely. Even more frustrating for the Delcassians, a former girlfriend of Niall's told Anne she'd overheard Niall and some other men talking about killing Irene. The girlfriend had even gone to Irene and warned her about it, she said, but nothing seemed to happen.

Then of course, Irene was murdered and the young woman

was too frightened to go to the police, in case the killers turned on her. In fact, shortly after her conversation with Anne, she fled abroad. Once again, Anne had run up against a brick wall.

And there, for years, the case remained stuck. The police could find no further clues. Apparently no new evidence appeared and it looked as if Irene's death would remain a tragic, unsolved mystery.

The Ice House was sold, the children went to live with their dad, and it was only Anne and Kenny, working tirelessly together over the years, who kept Irene's name and her fate alive in people's minds.

I heard from the couple from time to time. Anne organised a vigil outside The Ice House. There was a reconstruction of Irene's last movements on the morning she was killed. Anne went to speak to anyone and everyone she could think of who might know something about Irene's life. She listened to any theories, no matter how bizarre, and checked them out. She organised countless stories in the press, gave endless interviews and assisted in a number of documentaries about the baffling mystery. And she and Kenny kept in regular touch with the garda, passing on any titbits of information they'd managed to gather.

Despite it all, the years went by and nothing happened – except another tragedy. Anne was diagnosed with cancer, brought on I'm quite sure, by the stress of the case. But she wouldn't give up.

Then just over a decade later, a minor miracle happened. Out of the blue, a woman in Australia contacted the police after hearing about the case for the first time. Some years before, she'd dated a young Irish man she said, and one night, he confessed to her he'd once been paid to kill a woman. He hadn't wanted to do it, he said, but he was on drugs at the time, in debt to some scary people and desperate for money.

Presumably, this lady wasn't sure whether to believe him or

not, but his words stuck in her mind, and years later, when she heard about Irene's murder, she wondered if her ex-boyfriend could have been the killer.

The garda followed up her story and discovered that the boyfriend, one, Anthony Lambe, had suddenly dashed to England shortly after Irene's murder, and spent some time afterwards travelling around. More recently however, he'd returned to Ireland, and incredibly, at that moment, was currently a mature student at an Irish college, training to be a priest. .

When the police confronted him, Anthony Lambe confessed. He was very young, only 20 years old at the time, he said. He had been a penniless student, who worked part time as a security guard at Niall Power's security business for some extra cash. Someone had taken out a contract on Irene's life, he explained, and Niall – the go between – had recruited Anthony to do the evil deed. As he was desperately in debt, and frantic for cash, Anthony said yes.

Anthony turned out to be a heavily built, dark-haired man, exactly as I described in the vision Irene showed me, and he was very young at the time, just as I'd seen. How extraordinary that he was now trying to join the priesthood. I can only think the crime had weighed so heavily on his conscience ever since and he was trying to atone for his sins.

He was jailed for life in 2018, and incredibly, the day after he was sentenced, his boss, Niall Power walked into the police station and gave himself up.

Niall confessed to acting as the middleman and admitted he was the person who recruited young Anthony. Why? Well he was pressured constantly by the mastermind, he explained, to arrange Irene's killing, and in the end, he snapped and did as the mastermind asked. Despite it all, he was still too scared to name the person responsible.

Anne lived just long enough to have the satisfaction of seeing Niall Power sentenced to life imprisonment in July 2019. She passed away a month later, still regretting that the evil mastermind, the person ultimately responsible for three deaths – Irene, their mother Maureen and now Anne herself, was still walking free.

Of course, her husband Kenny promised her he'd keep up the fight and, good as his word, he had been carrying on for Anne ever since.

'And now it seems some new information's turned up, and the police are waiting to hear if there will be a trial,' said Kenny. 'It's just possible that after all this time, the mastermind will finally be brought to justice.'

'I hope so Kenny,' I said. 'I do hope so.'

That night as I was putting away the dishes, I was aware of Anne standing beside me.

'Whatever happens with the prosecution,' she said, 'that evil person hasn't got away with it. We're all together over here, haunting them!' she laughed. 'Me, Irene and Mum. We're working together – they get no peace.'

I couldn't help smiling. Anne hadn't lost her determined streak.

'I don't blame you,' I said. 'I think I'd do the same!'

'They thought they'd got away with it,' she went on, 'that they were so clever, but now nothing's going right for them. They're always looking over their shoulder and their health is fading. Right now they're suffering with bad digestive problems and it's going to get worse. One way or another, they're going to be very sorry... very sorry indeed...'

She moved away then, and I closed the cupboard door and headed for the sitting room. What an awful tragedy the whole thing had been. One vicious action had led to a whole family being wiped out, three children left motherless and even the Art Deco Ice House had been destroyed.

No one ever moved into it after it was sold, and it had fallen into such a bad state of disrepair, it was razed to the ground in 2016 to make way for a new development. The developers have promised that when the building work is complete, the site will include a memorial garden for Irene White. Let's hope they keep their word.

Nineteen

Oh no! I was so sleepy, but just as I was pulling back the duvet to get into bed I remembered I had a phone reading in the morning. It had completely slipped my mind.

Usually, if there's someone special a client wants to get in touch with, I ask them to send me a photograph first. That way I can spend a few minutes quietly linking with the loved one in advance, so that hopefully, by the time the reading begins, the channels of communication will be well and truly established.

Today though, rushing here, there and everywhere as usual, I'd totally forgotten to set the time aside, and now it was almost too late. I was so annoyed with myself. I knew tomorrow's client – a very sweet gentleman from the Netherlands – was desperate to speak to his lost daughter. I certainly didn't want to let him down. So, wearily, I dropped the duvet and padded out to find his daughter's picture.

There it was, downstairs on my desk. I picked it up and glanced at the happy snap. The photo actually showed two girls, sisters, but I could see straight away it was the younger one who was now in spirit. She looked very young, no more than seventeen, and she had beautiful long, dark hair and lively, mischievous eyes. The older sister was just as pretty but in a calmer, steadier way.

As I stared into the younger girl's eyes, a strong, youthful energy suddenly zoomed into the room.

'It's Dawn!' she said, right close to my ear. 'I can't wait to tell Daddy how much I love him. And I couldn't wait for you to speak to me Diane! I knew Dad was going to contact you.'

Wow! The link's established alright, I thought to myself.

Dawn was as eager to speak to her father as he was to speak to her. The reading should be fine tomorrow. I could go back to bed with a clear conscience.

So I put the picture back down on the desk, shut the door and off I went to the bedroom again. I slid in gratefully under the duvet, switched off the light and got myself comfortable. Ah, bliss.

The second I closed my eyes and started to drift off, Dawn was back.

'I can't wait to speak to him,' she whispered again. She was so excited about linking up with her Dad, she kept chattering to me all night.

'Tell Daddy I'm sorry,' She kept saying. 'I said things I shouldn't have done. Hurtful things. And I went off. I shouldn't have gone off. I'm so sorry. I was in a shack. They said I drowned. But I wouldn't have done. I'm a good swimmer. But something fell on me and I hurt my head.'

'Let's wait till tomorrow Dawn,' I said sleepily. 'Then you can talk to your dad properly.'

'Okay,' she finally agreed, 'but he knew I'd die young. I kept telling him.'

Not surprisingly, I was a bit bleary next morning, but I didn't mind because I knew we'd built up such a strong link, Dawn's dad wasn't going to be disappointed.

Sure enough, as soon as he came through on the video call, I could feel the air around me start to crackle with the familiar, bubbly energy Dawn radiated. You could see so much sadness in the poor man's eyes but Dawn was overjoyed to be able to pass her messages to him.

'Tell him I'm so, so sorry for everything I did wrong and said,' she kept saying.

'I was immature and I wanted to do everything because I thought I didn't have much time. I always thought I'd die young. I don't know why but I used to tell Dad I would.'

'Yes she did,' her father agreed. 'I could never understand it. I always asked her why she thought that but she said she didn't know. It was just a feeling.'

'I'm sorry, Dad. I said some hurtful things,' Dawn went on. 'I didn't mean it. We'd clash and I'd go off and cry and then think to myself "Well I'm going to die soon so I've got to make the most of my life" and I'd go and do something stupid.'

I got the impression Dawn was a typical rebellious teenager: mixing with the wrong people at times; drinking; maybe experimenting with a bit of wacky-baccy; arguing with her mum; leaving her room in a mess. All the kind of things so many teenagers do, then grow out of. But of course, Dawn never got the chance to grow out of it.

Suddenly, an image of Dawn's sister flashed into my mind.

'See how alike we look?' said Dawn. 'Tell her I love her too. She still cries for me, you know. She was always the good one. She was the one that listened to Mum and Dad. I was always stubborn. But tell her, now I can go and see her any time I want. I'm still there. I go to her flat and I've seen she's got a photo of the two of us by her bed.'

Dawn also explained that she visited her dad and stepmother regularly too. She knew they were moving house and she described her dad's study, even down to the picture on the wall.

'Completely accurate!' said her dad, in amazement.

'Well that's cos I've walked round it with him,' said Dawn. 'By the way, Dad's going to do very well in business and later on my sister is going to work with him. Something to do with design.'

'But what happened to you, Dawn?' I asked when she paused for a moment. 'Why did you pass away so young?'

'We were going away on a family holiday to Thailand, for Christmas,' said Dawn. 'It was a busy time but Dad managed to book us the last two rooms in the hotel. We were so excited. We thought it was a good omen. We thought it was meant to be. We thought we were so lucky.'

As she spoke, a shivery chill ran down my spine – and it wasn't the tragic irony of her words. This was starting to bring back memories of another reading from years ago that had a big impact on me.

'It wasn't the year of the tsunami, was it?' I asked.

'It was,' said Dawn. 'And it was my fault. Not the tsunami, but what happened to me. I should have stayed with the family. I'd have been okay if I stayed with them, but I didn't. I went off without them.'

I couldn't make out if perhaps she'd gone off with a boyfriend she'd met, or whether she was just exploring on her own, but the upshot was she ended up in a small building, some sort of wooden shack, when the wave hit.

'I'm a good swimmer,' said Dawn. 'If I'd been out in the open maybe I'd have been alright but I couldn't get out. Then something fell and hit me on the head. I was unconscious and I drowned.'

I had a brief, unsettling glimpse of Dawn drifting beneath the water, tendrils of dark hair floating around her like seaweed.

'My sister's going back to Thailand soon,' Dawn went on, brightly. 'She's going to put flowers on the sea and think of me. But I'll be there, standing beside her, trying to put my arm round her to comfort her. I don't want her to cry for me and be sad because I'm so happy where I am now. I'm doing all the things I was meant to do. I was meant to help other people from over here. I want them to understand there is life after death.'

It was a very emotional reading and Dawn had loving messages for her mother and stepmother, as well as her father and sister.

When it finally came to an end I was glad to think both Dawn's dad and Dawn herself were much happier.

But I was still vaguely distracted. Even as I put the phone down my mind was already flying back to the other, earlier reading that had jolted unexpectedly into my memory at the mention of the tsunami.

It was one of the strangest experiences I've ever had.

It started normally enough. It was back in the autumn of 2004. A very smart, well-spoken woman had booked a reading and she'd come along to my little office at the back of Peter's solicitor's practice. I can't recall now who she was trying to contact in particular, but things had been progressing quite normally. I was staring at my big white wall, watching the pictures the way I always do. After a while, the most beautiful scene unwound – I was looking at glorious white sand beaches, the bluest of blue seas, sparkling in the sun, and lush green foliage encircling perfect coves dotted with pretty, pastel buildings. 'This is where she lives,' the woman's contact said in my ear.

'Oh my goodness. You live in Paradise!' I said out loud. I could almost feel the warmth of that golden sun stroking my skin.

The woman laughed 'Yes. I suppose I do,' she agreed.

There was something familiar about the landscape. I stared again at the tiny boats drifting lazily towards a picture-postcard harbour, white sails billowing. I was still married to Peter at this point, and the scene reminded me very much of our dream wedding in Barbados. In fact, that bay looked very like one of the places we'd visited on our honeymoon.

'You don't live in Barbados do you?' I asked in surprise.

'As a matter of fact, I do,' said the woman. 'I'm over here visiting my mother at the moment, but I'll be going back soon.'

I was surprised, as she had no trace of a Caribbean accent, but the pictures never lie. Coincidentally enough, Peter and I had enjoyed Barbados so much, Peter had just booked us a return trip in a few months' time. We were planning a beach Christmas – a second honeymoon during the festive season. I could hardly wait.

The reading went on as normal, with some interesting messages for the client's daughter, but then suddenly, for no reason I could work out, the atmosphere seemed to change. I was being shown a glorious beach scene again but now it didn't feel like paradise. There was something very 'not right' going on. My heart started to thud in anxiety. Something seriously alarming was going to happen, I knew it, and I couldn't tear my eyes away.

As I watched, the sea seemed to pull right back off the sand, exposing the seabed and leaving puzzled sunbathers and swimmers, laughing and pointing out the strange phenomenon to one another.

But over their heads in the distance, I could see a menacing line of dark blue appear on the horizon, and it seemed to be growing taller and taller, blotting out the sky. At first, few people noticed it, but then I realised it was moving, racing towards the beach. A vast, towering wall of water accelerating towards the shore, devouring everything in its path.

All at once, the sunbathers' baffled expressions turned to screams, and everyone was running in panic towards the village. Most didn't make it. The giant wave crashed right over them and continued tearing inland bowling over hotels, waterside restaurants and palm trees. Everything disappeared under the glassy avalanche.

Then the wall picture dissolved, to be replaced by images of quiet devastation. Water, water everywhere. The tops of submerged buildings parted the waves, bodies bobbing slowly between them. Uprooted trees and debris drifted to and fro and I could see Christmas trees and Christmas decorations floating beneath the surface, tinsel streaming after them.

I was utterly horrified. I didn't know what to make of the horrendous disaster unfolding before my eyes. We'd been talking about the woman's daughter when the vision began so I could only assume this must be a warning for her.

'There's a big wave,' I began, because back then I don't think I'd even heard the word tsunami before so I had no other name for it. 'A huge wave.' I was so disturbed it was difficult to find a way to explain what I'd seen. 'Please tell your daughter to be very, very careful. She mustn't go near a beach over the Christmas period.'

My client was a bit taken aback by my alarmed expression.

'That's okay,' she said. 'Nothing to worry about. My daughter lives in Canada. She's not planning to visit over Christmas.'

'That's good,' I said. 'Please tell her not to travel around Christmas time and stay away from the beach yourself.'

The woman was puzzled but promised to pass on the warning and take great care.

After she'd left, the images kept playing on in my mind. I couldn't get those drowned Christmas decorations out of my head. I was being shown that the disaster would happen at Christmas time, that was perfectly clear, and as I'd previously been shown pictures of Barbados, and my client was from Barbados, I assumed the island was where the tsunami would hit.

But maybe the warning hadn't been for my client's daughter, I thought suddenly, maybe it had been for me! After all, we were heading for that very island, that very Christmas. I was so shaken I phoned Peter straight away and persuaded him to change the dates of our holiday. He was a bit surprised at my request and found it hard to believe my vision could possibly come true. By now though, he had faith in my psychic abilities and reckoned it was better to be safe than sorry.

So we gave up on our sunshine Christmas and took our trip to Barbados a few weeks earlier than planned. Yet despite the change of dates, I was still uneasy. I started to panic every time I was in the sea and the waves began getting choppy, and though I love the beach as much as anyone, that holiday I made sure we spent most of our time sightseeing!

Thankfully, despite my nerves, everything went smoothly. Barbados was as lovely as ever and there were no unpleasant surprises. We came home safe and sound, ready to enjoy a Welsh Christmas with the family. Maybe I was wrong, I thought, as I unpacked our things with relief and began preparing to put up the Christmas tree.

Maybe I'd seen visions of some Christmas disaster way in the future. Maybe there was no need to worry right now. So why was that uncomfortable feeling still burrowing down deep in my stomach? It was there, beneath the laughter and festivities on Christmas Day and, if anything, on Boxing Day it was slightly worse. I tried to ignore it and tell myself it was just my imagination. That everything was fine.

Then, around teatime on the 26th, we switched on the TV to see the awful news that a tsunami had just struck a number of countries in the Indian Ocean, including Thailand. Open-mouthed, I stared as the horrifying scenes I'd watched on my wall months before, began unrolling across the TV screen. 100 ft waves, we were told, had ripped through beachside communities around the region and thousands of people had been killed. The death toll was later estimated to be around a quarter of a million. It was an unimaginable catastrophe.

Peter turned pale as one devastating scene followed another on the TV. 'Oh My God Diane,' he said at last, 'It looks like you were right. Only it wasn't Barbados.'

It gave me no pleasure to have my fears vindicated.

In the months that followed, the incident continued to trouble me, and not just because of the magnitude of the tragedy. Why had the vision interrupted a perfectly normal reading? I wondered. Particularly as it seemed to have no relevance to my client's life, or even to mine. It had arrived, unbidden from nowhere, with no warning. I couldn't understand it. How did this premonition come to be shown to me, and why?

In the end it was Grandfather who put my mind at rest. He appeared at the end of the bed one morning, as I was brushing my hair and pondering for the hundredth time what that tsunami message had been about. After all there was no way I could have stopped it...

'Diane,' interrupted Grandfather gently, fixing me with his compelling dark eyes, 'you're still learning, still mastering your gift. And your gift is growing – developing in many different directions. But you must let it unfold naturally, like a flower opening. Don't worry or fret or try to force things. Just relax, trust in us, and everything will fall into place as it's meant to do.'

It wasn't the answer to my question exactly, but his words soothed me. As his features gradually faded and disappeared, I realised I felt calmer. I put down the brush and collected up my things ready for the day.

At last I could see what he was getting at. Okay, so still I didn't understand why I'd been shown the tsunami in advance, but right now I didn't need to understand. I just had to go with the flow, do my best to learn from whatever happened, and pass on any information I received, honestly. One day, the pieces of the jigsaw would fit together and everything would be clear, but right now all I had to do was accept.

Strangely enough, as I headed into the office later that day, I had the oddest feeling there was something else my Grandfather wanted me to know but that morning hadn't been quite the right time.

Oh well, I thought, as I tidied my office for the next client, I won't worry about it now. I'll follow his advice and go with the flow. He'll tell me when he's good and ready.

As it turned out, I didn't have too long to wait. A few nights later, Dean and I sat down to watch an old film on TV. The Ghost and the Darkness it was called, starring Michael Douglas and Val Kilmer. I'd heard about this film before but hadn't had a chance to catch it until now. What intrigued me, was that it was based on the story of the killer lions of Tsavo and the exploits of Colonel John Patterson – as told by Colonel Patterson himself, in a book he wrote about the incident a few years afterwards: The Man Eaters of Tsavo.

I suppose I shouldn't have been surprised that the Colonel was the hero of his own book, and he credited himself with hunting down and killing the terrifying beasts. After my visit to the Tsavo lodge in Kenya with Mike a few years before, I knew this was the version that had gone down in history and my grandfather didn't get a mention.

Yet once again, as the film got under way and the events of the building of the railway, so realistically recreated on screen, began unrolling, I found myself growing more and more agitated, just like I did in Kenya. Grandfather was close by and he was not happy.

'It's a travesty,' he kept saying in my ear, and I knew he was scowling at the TV, as the film wound on, 'a travesty! Why do they do this? I'll tell you how it was Diane,, and it will help you understand your gift and where it comes from.'

It was clear I wasn't going to be able to follow the film, so I settled back to listen to him.

'I was already working on the railway when Patterson arrived,' said my grandfather. 'We'd been there for months. He only came to help with a bridge. He had skills as a bridge builder but he didn't know Africa, he didn't know the soil and he didn't understand the workers.

'So he arrived one day with his own men, all carrying his fine china, and his bath and his clothes that he insisted on changing daily. He was an aristocrat who looked down on my workers – the hard-working men who'd been there from day

One. He shouted at them, spoke down to them and wouldn't eat with them. He even tried to stop them praying.

It was a huge challenge to build the railway across that land, so I learned to work alongside the men and ask their opinions. Treat people the way you like to be treated, is what I've always believed. I had a psychic gift, and those who have nothing materially and no education, often have valuable skills too. These men I worked with had learned to use the abilities of their senses because they have nothing else. That's a priceless gift.

The land was so difficult, I realised I'd need to use my psychic skills, plus those of the workers, to help get the tracks laid. So every night when the sky was dark and full of stars, I'd sit and visualise what we needed to do the next day and I encouraged my workers to do the same.

It was a form of meditation. Visualisation is very powerful and it became an essential tool.

I'd have a hundred men sitting under the stars, all visualising the land ahead: mountains, earth like orange dust, not enough equipment... We would sit in silence, in the darkness, and visualise what needed to be done the following day and how we could achieve it.

When I closed my eyes, I could see where things would go; I visualised what the soil would be like further down. I saw clearly the rocks that would be a problem, how we would find a way to blast them, even though we didn't have the right tools, and I got input from my workers who also had vision, even though they had no education and few possessions.

We did this visualising every evening and the information we received allowed us to build the next section of track. Then Patterson took the credit!

My psychic skills were useful in other ways too. If we needed new workers, I would read their palms and I could see right away which men would be honest and hard-working, and which untrustworthy. I was so often right that in the end when anything in the camp was stolen, as sometimes happened, the suspects were sent to me to find out which ones were guilty.

As for the lions, when we got to Tsavo, they arrived. Creeping quietly into the camp in a pack at night, when everyone was sleeping, taking all these young boys first. Young boys aged just 12 to 16, sleeping together on straw mats. The weakest first.

The boys didn't even get the chance to scream, or shout out. They couldn't. The lions were so intelligent, they pierced their victim's throats with their teeth first, then dragged them out of their tents. After the most vulnerable boys, the lions started on the men. There were always men missing in the morning, disappeared so silently in the dark that people began to whisper they must have been taken by ghosts or devils.

I took to sitting up all night with a rifle and a couple of companions keeping watch. I actually shot one of the man-eaters, but there were more of them and the disappearances went on. Eventually, I had to move up the line to progress another area of track, and Patterson stayed behind at the camp and shot the last two lions. That's what really happened. Though no one knows it today.

When the line was eventually finished, I moved to Nairobi. It was just being created from barren swampland at the time, but I loved Africa, I wanted to stay, and we became pioneers, building a brand new city.

I opened a shop in the new main street and bought some farmland. But I was still interested in psychic matters and the development of psychic powers. I gave readings in the back of the shop, just like you do Diane, and I helped open a psychic centre in the town – an African branch of the Theosophical Society, which remains a worldwide organisation to this day. Above all, I wanted to prove there was life after death. And now that's what I want to help you do, Diane. That's why I have been by your side your whole life.'

Wow! Across the room I could see the credits beginning to roll on the TV screen but they were all misty and I realised my eyes were full of tears. I'd missed the entire film but it didn't matter a bit. My Grandfather had just given me the most important message I'd ever received. The meaning and purpose of my life.

I felt quite overwhelmed. Dean turned towards me but I couldn't speak.

Then I felt an invisible hand fall gently on my shoulder. 'Don't cry child,' said my Grandfather softly, 'Dry your eyes. We've got work to do. This is just the beginning.'

My Great Great Grandparents.
Yes, he is my wonderful guide, my lined man & my Grandma
Florence in the African bush
& always by my side…

And Finally...

Thank you so much for reading this far. I do hope you've enjoyed the book. I want to say a big thank you to everyone who's contributed to these pages and huge apologies to those whose wonderful stories could not be included, due to lack of space.

As I'm often unable to recall the details of many of the readings I do, I asked if any clients who'd like to be in the book could help by sending me their memories. I've been deluged with replies! And I've been so touched by your kind words. It's a great shame I've been unable to include them all. I think I shall just have to write another book!

Anyway, here are just a tiny few of the letters I would love to have added to these chapters...

Dear Diane,

My son Nick died in an accident in London 12 years ago, which was absolutely devastating for the family. I'd never had a reading with a medium before but felt very strongly that I needed to have one. My daughter bought me your book and as soon as I read it I knew that I really needed to see you. I rang and was absolutely delighted to be offered a reading within 8 weeks of Nick's passing because someone had been unable to keep their appointment.

The reading was simply astounding. This is what happened:

Nick came through immediately and Diane told me that he was communicating really strongly. She described him very accurately, including his nature. Through Diane, he was able to tell us how the accident happened and reassured me that he was fine. Typical of Nick, he said that the accident had come as a bit of a shock to him as well as to the family.

Before the accident, the whole family, including our grandchildren, had all booked to go to Disney World in Florida. Through Diane, he told me that he would be there with us all, saying that he wouldn't even have to pay the airfare.

His humour and wit in the reading was exactly as it always was, he even said,

"Tell Mum I've met Michael Jackson."

The reading was so reassuring to the whole family.

I had another reading with Diane in Birmingham, in the January prior to the Covid lockdown. Nick came through immediately and talked about his sister and his nieces and mentioned his sister's husband. I said that I was not too sure about him. He immediately stated that the husband was having an affair which had been going on for about nine months. My daughter had no clue whatsoever.

Nick said the husband had known this woman from years before he met my daughter and told us that she was 49 years old, blonde, and worked in an office.

In the reading Nick told me that the husband was lying to my daughter all the time and that he had massive debts. All of this proved to be true and my daughter immediately started divorce proceedings when she confronted him and he admitted everything. Had I not had the reading with Diane his affair would have carried on and he would have built up even more debts. We found this amazing.

Through Diane, Nick also told me that I was having digestive problems which was absolutely true. He told me that I might need to go into hospital and told me that all the nurses will be wearing full protective covering with masks etc.

Diane said to me that she couldn't really understand this as my condition didn't warrant that kind of protective clothing. It was only later we realised what he was talking about. By the time my operation came round, Covid 19 had struck and all the nursing staff had to wear full PPE protection. Nick had predicted it.

I now know that what Diane tells me in the readings that I have had with her is stunningly accurate.

Dear Diane,

I've had a few readings since my brother's passing in 2018. It has helped me and my family tremendously knowing he didn't suffer when he died. You were able to explain how he died (slipped whilst walking a local mountain) but that's he's happy. Knowing my brother is still with us and is happy gives us great comfort.

You mentioned family members and described their personalities to a tee. You even mentioned my brother's name during the reading- which you couldn't have known.

During one reading you explained that my brother was glad he didn't spend money on a van he recently purchased a few months prior to his passing and mentioned a campervan conversion. This is exactly true. I was in disbelief. My brother had bought a new van with a plan on converting it into a campervan – something he had already done on his previous camper. You also asked why my brother was referring to me by another name (my middle name which you were unaware of) and said my middle name out loud. My whole family including my brother are the only ones who refer to me by this name.

These are only a few examples of the comfort and reassurance you've given us with your readings. Things that couldn't be known by anyone!

Dear Diane,

I've come for a few readings with you and have always been fascinated by how accurate you have been with details about my past and present, including naming/describing family members and discussing events. More fascinating to me is your ability to predict my future. So many things have come true over the years, there have been too many to list them all, but one that has been most prominent is that you said my mother would injure her back in January, and 18 months later on Jan 13th my mum fractured her spine! You have predicted exact names and events.

After my readings you have always asked me to give you feedback. I've always waited, but after another of your predictions came true today, I had to let you know! I'm always amazed, and it actually is very comforting and offers a lot of hope. Many thanks Diane!

Nic xx

Dear Diane,

Just have to tell you about some things that you predicted have come true, just because I find it astonishing how the predictions unfold! About five years ago you told me in a reading that I would move house, and the house would be next to a friend who was a 'blonde teacher friend.'

Well, three years ago I moved house and there was no teacher friend next to me. At that point I had absolutely no intention of moving again, but then this year I ended up moving again! And the house just happened to be right next door to my blonde friend, who is a teacher!

Also in my mother's reading this year, you told her some aspects of my future. They turned out to be the same exact points that you had said in my reading and there's no way you could have known we knew each other. During that reading, you told my mother that 'her daughter's friend would be driving a white car' – the daughter being me. Well, my friend came to visit today, and she turned up in her brand new white car! You also said that my work would involve more disabilities and August would link to a course, well I am about to start a new job working with disabilities and I have to do a course in August as part of it! That's just a few of the things.

Dear Diane,

I just wanted to give you some feedback from the recent burning question response I received from you.

I'd asked for information regarding my husband's health. I was reluctant to give any information away to you as I wanted to see if you would pick up on what's happened.

Immediately you mentioned his heart and fat around the heart.

A year ago on the 6th of July, my husband had a heart attack at the age of 51 and ended up having double bypass surgery. You also mentioned pains in his knees. He's actually suffering with vascular disease and suffers with awful pains in his legs when walking. You said he saw me as his 'Florence Nightingale'. I am a nurse and I sort all his medication and arrange his hospital appointments. You even recognised the fact he was in a previous bad relationship before we met! You are truly amazing and have provided me with much needed reassurance, as I worry about him daily – understandably.

I don't know how you do it, and over the years I have had several readings with you and you never fail to amaze me! I even played the recording for my husband!

When life is busy and you don't have time to come for a full reading, but that burning question is bugging you, this is truly a blessing.

Diolch Diane for all you do, you certainly are one very special lady,

Take care,

Amanda

Dear Diane,

The first time I saw you was shortly after I lost my baby boy. You said to me that I would have an operation to have a baby, but we were adamant that we couldn't. Because of my incompetent cervix, my last 2 pregnancies only got to 24 weeks, and we couldn't face losing any more babies.

Unfortunately my doctors didn't know much about this condition, which is called transabdominal cervical cerclage (TAC). Because of this we didn't even think about trying again, but you were so right. I was referred to the right doctor and a year later l had the operation. You were even right about where the hospital was. As that particular hospital was 50 miles from my home, I couldn't believe you were right, but you were.

A few months after the operation, I fell pregnant and I gave birth to my beautiful daughter at 29 weeks. We weren't too sure she was going to survive, due to being in distress and being left on and off oxygen for 14 hours during the birth, but you told me she'd survive, and that I'd sue the hospital for negligence and poor medical care as my daughter has been left with cerebral palsy.

I won the case, just as you said I would. You even mentioned how much compensation we would get, and you were right again! Now we have enough money to help with anything she needs for the rest of her life and to buy a nice house specially adapted.

You told me my life would change so much, that I would move and I would be so much happier in who I was as a person. You told me that I would be pushing a wheelchair in years to come. You also told me that I wouldn't stay with my husband at the time. We are divorced now and have been for a few years. I'm with someone else, my baby girl is now 9 years of age and full of smiles. She can sit for a bit, she can't walk or talk but she's definitely the heart of our home. Just looking at her brightens up my whole life.

Thank you so much,

Sofia

Dear Diane,

You were right I am pregnant just like you visualised & it's also a boy.

Dear Diane,

I was so upset to lose my dog Charlie but you said he's there by your feet. In fact, he used to always sleep lying over your left foot. My God Diane, I can't believe you said those words – that's exactly what he did. I used to have pins and needles in my left foot but I wouldn't move it if I could help it in case it woke him up.

You also told me he was a rescue dog and he didn't have a good life before I took him in. You had a vision of a man standing over him with a stick and I'd noticed that Charlie was afraid of men. Once a man came to the door holding an umbrella in his hand and Charlie was cowering down.

You also told me not to regret that I'd had to have him put down due to bad stomach problems. He would have suffered so much that I definitely did the right thing at the right time. It gave me a lot of comfort to know that.

Dear Diane,

I came to one of your theatre shows and you gave me messages from my father. At one point he was talking about my son and said something about my son's brightly coloured wallet. I was puzzled at this and couldn't think what he meant. When I got home I asked my son what colour his wallet was and he said, 'black'. But some time later he was looking through a drawer and found an old brightly coloured wallet he'd had for years that he'd forgotten about. He opened it up and found a pound note inside that had been given to him by his Grandad. He'd always kept that pound note and not spent it because his Grandad had given it to him.

Dear Diane,

This morning I just came across a fertility question I asked you from 21/07/2015. OMG, so accurate! You said, in 3 years' time I will have my son – well exactly 3 years on (minus one day) he was born. You even described his personality spot on, including small details like the fact you could see him running on my wood flooring. It brought back the raw feelings of infertility whilst listening to it, but I know it gave me the reassurance I needed to keep going.

Thanks a million.

Annika

Dear Diane,

Six years ago you told me I'd open my own spa and that it would 'work'. In fact I'd have a chain of spas. I didn't believe it as I'd always thought I'd work for someone else. I didn't think I had it in me to run my own business.

Well after the reading, it got me thinking and I started doing business plans and attending beauty shows. It had always been a dream of mine since childhood to be really successful in business, not because of the money but just to know I'd done something great before passing on into the next life.

Well since that reading six years ago I've launched my first spa and last month I opened my second. I can't believe I've done it and I want to open more. So my message to everyone out there is if you have a dream follow it and believe in yourself.

Thank you Diane because if I hadn't had that reading with you – would I be in the position I'm in today?

Tara

Acknowledgements

I want to thank my lovely friend Linda Dearsley for her wonderful patience and her natural, gifted ability to string words together in the way she does, that made this book possible.

Linda is not only my wonderful friend, she was introduced to me by the great medium, Doris Stokes. Doris had already passed on by that time, but she's clearly still continuing her work from the Spirit World. She wanted Linda to help me with my book so, she organised for us to meet and we've been friends ever since.

Linda explained the writing process to me like this: 'Diane, creating a good book is like stringing a necklace of beautiful pearls. Every section has to fit together perfectly or the necklace will be spoiled.'

I love her words & I am sure you will all love her natural way of writing, stringing my story together like a lovely pearl necklace.

I also want to thank my wonderful children Lisa & Liam. We have been through so much together yet we are all so strong & I'm proud of you both.

We've all learned along the way that no matter what life throws at you it can only make you stronger. The struggle and hard times simply teach you to appreciate life even more.

I also want to thank my Great, Great Grandad and Grandmother for sharing their lives with me from the Spirit World and teaching me how to use the natural gifts I was born with.

Most importantly I want to thank the strongest woman I know, for giving me life and for helping me grow. Although she worried for me as a child, my wonderful mum Pat now understands my gift and has given me confidence to use it.

Then there's the best sister you could wish for, Debbie, who told me straight when I was ready to run away: 'Diane you **can** stand in front of a theatre full of people!' And I did too - with Debbie by my side, as she has been whenever I need her.

And not forgetting my dependable brother Steve, always ready to lend a hand and of course Gary, the wonderful big brother who's helped me countless times and has been looking out for me since I was a skinny little girl. You'll always be my hero, Gary. You went to the Falklands and came back a Hero.

And last but by no means least, the amazing man I love, Dean. Always smiling, always making me laugh and bringing back joy to my life when I least suspected it.

Thank you all.

*Available worldwide from
Amazon and all good bookstores*

www.mtp.agency

www.facebook.com/mtp.agency

@mtp_agency

www.ingramcontent.com/pod-product-compliance
Lightning Source LLC
LaVergne TN
LVHW021703060526
838200LV00050B/2480